AUSCHWITZ
to AUSTRALIA

AUSCHWITZ *to* AUSTRALIA

A Holocaust Survivor's Memoir

OLGA HORAK

Jagar Sprinting

with my very best wishes and thanks of or visiting the Sydney Jewish Museum

Olga Horak

Sydney.
6. Nov. 2012.

First published in Australia in 2000 by Kangaroo Press
An imprint of Simon & Schuster (Australia) Pty Limited
20 Barcoo Street, East Roseville NSW 2069

A Viacom Company
Sydney New York London Toronto Tokyo Singapore

National Library of Australia
Cataloguing-in-Publication data

Horak, Olga
Auschwitz to Australia.

ISBN 0-975 1092-6-X

1. Horak, Olga. 2. Holocaust survivors – Australia –
Biography. 3. Holocaust, Jewish (1939–1945) – Slovakia –
5. Slovaks – Australia – Biography. I. Title.

940.5318092

Cover and internal design by Anna Soo Design
Front cover, left to right: Olga Horak's parents, Hugo and Piroska; Olga and John Horak;
Cyrenia, the ship that brought Olga and John to Australia. The telegram pictured was sent
by Olga on 26 October 1945.
Back cover: Judith and Olga Rosenberger

Set in 13/16 pt Bembo
Printed in Australia by Jagar Pty Ltd t/as Jagar Sprinting

10 9 8 7 6 5 4 3 2

Lovingly dedicated to the memory
of my beloved parents
Hugo and Piroska Rosenberger
and sister
Judith Rosenberger

My eternal love to my husband
John

And to my daughters
Evelyn and Susie

And to my grandchildren
Kirsty, Anthony and Jonathan

Contents

Acknowledgments

Writing my story has been a long process over many years. For a long time I remained silent, as did many survivors. However, I believe it is important to record the testimonies of those who, like me, did survive the Holocaust, so that the next generation will know and our stories will not be lost. In putting my story together, I was fortunate to have the help and assistance of many people to whom I owe a debt of gratitude and thanks.

To Janice Beavan I express my thanks for her patience and expertise in preparing the typescript from my diaries.

I thank Eva Engel, a wonderful community worker who introduced me to Professor Colin Tatz and his wife Sandra. They encouraged me to speak publicly as a Holocaust survivor and because of this I began to record my testimony. To both Colin and Sandra I say thank you.

My special gratitude goes to Paul O'Shea. Paul extended a helping hand through his compassion and understanding of the history of the Holocaust. He gave his time to help me revise and edit the manuscript. Paul's gifts as an historian and theologian served as great supports. His friendship is greatly appreciated.

I thank my publishers Simon & Schuster, in particular Brigitta Doyle for her guidance during the editing process and Camilla Dorsch for her marketing expertise.

My final thanks go to Ernie Friedlander, from B'nai B'rith in Sydney, for his tireless support and generosity.

Foreword

Recording the testimony of survivors of the Holocaust has become more urgent as the years pass. The witnesses to the Shoah are growing older and, as that happens, our link with the events of that period of human history grow tenuous. It is important therefore to record and remember, not only for the sake of generations to come, but in order to create as complete a history as possible.

Survivor testimony is an important source for our knowledge and understanding of the Holocaust. It provides the historian and general reader with an 'insiders' experience of events that are often felt to be so far removed from 'ordinary' human life as to be almost from another planet. And herein lies a potential danger. Testimony must be read in conjunction with formal histories of the Holocaust so that the reader gains a global picture that places the survivor within a context.

No two survivors' stories are the same. Olga Horak's testimony is a moving account of a young girl maturing into womanhood during the years of fascist and Nazi oppression in Slovakia. Many of the events she recounts occurred when Olga was in her early teenage years. Readers need to remind themselves that Olga's memories are those of a young girl emotionally unprepared for the horrors unleashed upon her and her family. Her story is precisely that – it is Olga's story. One of the effects of the Holocaust on her life was the fact that she was banned from attending school classes because she was Jewish. Consequently readers may find Olga's style different from others – but her experience was shaped within such parameters. Rather than diminish her testimony, Olga's written style reminds us of the awful power wielded by those who engineered and executed the 'Final Solution'.

It has been my task as an editorial adviser to make suggestions in order to clarify details and help locate dates and places. The story remains Olga's and it is her voice that rings throughout the text.

My collaboration with Olga has been a rich and fruitful experience for me over several years. I have marvelled at the resilience of her spirit and in particular her determination to honour the memory of her parents and sister through undertaking this task. Olga is indeed a woman of valour, and I am humbled to think she calls me friend.

PAUL O'SHEA PhD

CHAPTER ONE

The New Order 1939-1942

LIFE CHANGED FOR my family in a series of rapid strokes after the passing of the Nuremberg Laws in Slovakia. We lived in Bratislava and I was thirteen when the war broke out. Judith, my sister, was fourteen. My mother, Piroska, was thirty-four and my father, Hugo Rosenberger, was forty-five. My father and uncles conducted their livestock business from the family house in Miczkiewicova Ulica 16/Spitalska Ulica 45. Omama, my father's mother, lived on the ground floor. However, many of my friends and relatives were leaving Slovakia. My Aunt Irene and Uncle Karl and their family left for Palestine in early 1939, joining many other Jewish families who wanted to get out of Europe. Among them was my childhood girlfriend Jutzi Kann. People often ask, 'Why did you not leave too?' How can one answer that question? We simply had no idea, could not even begin to imagine what was to happen to us. Germany was the most cultured country in Europe, the home of so many great figures in European history. We had lived well with our Christian neighbours in Bratislava and Slovakia for years.

Who could imagine that this was to change overnight? And if we left, who would look after those who could not leave? Omama was nearly eighty; Grandmother Ilona, my mother's mother, was too old to travel. Could you leave your loved ones? The answer for my parents was 'No'.

In 1940 the first anti-semitic laws directly affected my sister Judith and me. We were unable to continue our schooling at the Zivnodom, the exclusive German-speaking high school for girls. Now, learning practical skills became essential. Judith and I attended classes learning how to sew, make leather belts, artificial silk flowers and machine embroidery.

My mother also enrolled in courses, learning how to make cakes and chocolates from Guderna, the well-established confectioner. She became quite an expert and tried out new recipes at home. This delighted us. Mother foresaw the need for us to acquire as many skills as possible. The changes that suddenly began to occur all around us proved her right.

Under the dismemberment of Czechoslovakia, Bohemia and Moravia became a *Reichsprotektorat* ruled from Prague. Slovakia was supposedly independent under the rule of Monsignor Josef Tiso. Hungary had demanded and been given a large slice of southern Slovakia, including Grandmother Ilona's home in Sala which meant that our holidays with her were now ended. Grandmother buried some of her valuables in various places about Sala. I found some of them years later; others remain buried where she left them. I never saw her again.

In Bratislava, the anti–semitic laws made life difficult for us. My parents were ordered, by government decree, to hand over property and valuables. My father's farm at the Majerhof was 'Aryanised', as was the family business in the city. The 'Aryan' who took over the official management was Mr Suhajda, a decent man who had been a boxer and freestyle fighter. His wife was an aristocratic lady who offered to take and protect some of my parent's valuables. Mother and father were wary about what they handed over. Under the new laws Jews were forbidden to own diamond rings and earrings, gold bracelets, chains, or watches. Radios had to be handed in, along with furs and silverware. My parents entrusted some things to close friends and even managed to send some valuables out of the country. A distant cousin of my father's looked after a safe deposit box in London, and another relative opened an account in New York where father had been sending money for some time. It is even possible that he opened a Swiss bank account since he travelled frequently to St Margarethen.

We were ordered to wear the Star of David stitched firmly on our outer clothing. It was not pleasant and, although I was not ashamed to wear the star, I was endangered on the street where some people abused me with foul language and bodily harm. Strangers spat at me. I learnt quickly to carry my bag or books high on my chest to cover the star. If I was caught doing that I would have been in trouble for not having the star displayed. At the time, I was only fourteen and had lived a very peaceful and sheltered existence up until then. I had grown up in a home filled with warmth, love and happiness. As a child, I thought our family would always be safe – with Omama, Grandmother Ilona, my uncles and aunts, cousins and friends – we would always be together. Now, all Jews had to be indoors by sunset; we were forbidden to sit on park benches, go to cinemas or visit public places. I felt deprived. I couldn't understand all the hatred. What had I ever done to deserve such treatment? What had my parents done? Fear became a part of my life and it gnawed at me all the time.

Many young Jewish men and single women registered with local Zionist groups to prepare for the illegal journey to Palestine. Ships were hired and sailed from Bratislava's wharf heading down the Danube towards the Black Sea where ocean liners should have taken them to Palestine. The Hungarian authorities frequently refused to issue the ships with transit visas and consequently the ships lay stranded between the borders of Slovakia and Hungary for weeks on end. My father and other members of the Jewish community often drove in his car to the border taking food, blankets and tents. It was a very dangerous undertaking as by now Jews were forbidden to have 'unessential' contact with non-Jews.

SS Sturmbannführer Dieter Wislizeny was sent on instructions from Berlin to act as an 'adviser' to the Slovakian government on implementing its anti-Jewish policies. He arrived in Bratislava with a detachment of SS troops. It is hard to describe the feeling of terror I experienced whenever I saw their black uniform. I froze and couldn't move. I used to feel sick in the pit of my stomach. All I knew was that I had to get away from them as quickly as I could.

Wisliczeny worked in close collaboration with a number of high-ranking Nazis whose mission was to complete the 'Final Solution' in Central Europe. *SS Obersturmbannführer* Adolf Eichmann, head of the Reich Central Security Office desk in Jewish Affairs was responsible for the coordination of the extermination process across Nazi-occupied Europe. He answered directly to the *Reichsführer SS* Heinrich Himmler. Ernst Kaltenbrunner, the State Secretary for Internal Security in Vienna was a vicious anti-semite who was promoted because of his hatred of Jews. In January 1943 he succeeded the murdered *Reichsprotektor* Heydrich as head of the Reich Central Security Office. *SS Hauptsturmführer* Alois Brunner had won his superiors high praise for his ruthlessness and success as a much-feared 'Jew hunter'. It was the work of these men in the murky and shadowy world of the Nazi regime that meant the death of thousands of Slovakian Jews, among them most of my family.*

With keen precision Wislizeny and his fellow anti-semites manipulated and encouraged a willing Slovakian government to gradually strip all Jews of all their rights, property and protection. We were demoralised, humiliated and reduced to thinking of ourselves as less than human. As we were not allowed to employ non-Jews we had to say farewell to our dear maid Anna. She found work with the family of the Slovakian Interior Minister Alexander (Sano) Mach. Several days later, Anna came to us crying. Mach had raped her the first day she worked in his house.

---

*For a more detailed analysis of the political situation in Europe at this time see the Appendix.

My father and uncles worked for Mr Suhajda in the office for a short time, mainly to teach him how to conduct the business and look after the livestock on the farm. Mr Suhajda, who now owned the livestock business, looked very prosperous. He drove my father's car and he had become known in business circles.

My parents held many meetings with all members of the family. Discussions, conferences, secrets and codes were established behind closed doors. My mother's relatives, the Friedlieb family, visited frequently as did my grandmother Ilona's brother Maurice Friedlieb, cousin Dr Alexander Friedlieb and the Bardos family. The Bardos family was close to my mother and played a very important part in my life after the war.

In 1941 before the first transports to Auschwitz started there were the *Kindertransports*. These were last-ditch attempts by Jewish parents to send their children to safety out of reach of the Nazis. My Uncle Bibi Stern was instrumental in setting up these transports and was able to send two of his seven children, Kurt and Harry to England. Once in London they were placed in foster care with non-Jewish families who provided them with love and care. My parents along with the rest of the family agreed that Judith and I were not to be sent on our own. We would stay together as a family.

On 21 March 1942 a new anti-semitic law was passed which struck a terrible blow to all Jewish families and particularly to mine. All single Jews born before or in 1925 were ordered to report to the Slovakian authorities and be registered for forced labour. It was pronounced loud and clear that 'It will be good for the Jews to finally do some work'. Those to be conscripted were told they could take a rucksack with some necessities and some food. On 22 March, in the evening after the Jewish curfew had begun, two Hlinka guards (the fascists home guard in Slovakia) came to our house, compared and checked documents about Judith and then ordered her to report to the old Patronka ammunition factory the next morning. Patronka was next to an old abandoned railway line about ten kilometres outside Bratislava. We were stunned. Judith did not know how to react. She was very brave and began to pack, I imagine she was in shock. My mother cried and my father tried to pacify her even though he must have felt desperate. I was in shock and sat in a corner and waited for something to happen.

My father went immediately to look up an old friend who now held an important position in the Hlinka Guard and was a minister in Tiso's government. Father had known him through business contacts for many years. He had always said to my father, 'Dear friend Hugo, if you ever need anything at all, call on me and I will help.' My father remembered his words and was convinced that now was the time to ask for help. My father returned home, sad, downhearted and disappointed. His eyes filled with tears. He told us that he fell to his knees and begged: 'Please help me. My child is being taken away.' But the man remained unmoved and cold. He replied to my father: 'Sorry, but I cannot help you.'

My mother was shattered. I was incredibly sad and depressed, withdrawn and did not speak to anyone. I do not think that anyone noticed how lonely and miserable and affected I was. My sister Judith and four cousins,

Magda, Eva, Fritz and Erwin, were going away and none of us knew what was going to happen to them. The tension and anxiety of not knowing is perhaps worse than anything else. What would happen to my sister? Where was she going? Would she ever come home? And what of my cousins? We knew that deportations were taking place. Trains headed 'to the East' but what happened to them, we did not know, except that it was not good. No one ever thought that they would be killed. No, that was unthinkable – that would be inhuman!

The next morning, 25 March, Judith, Magda, Eva, Fritz and Erwin reported to the 'Gathering Place' at Patronka. They left that day with 995 other teenage Jewish boys and girls. We did not know it then, but they were heading straight to Auschwitz. To the best of my knowledge my sister and cousins were ordered out of the transport at the new Auschwitz II – better known to the world as Birkenau. My sister Judith was probably murdered about two weeks before her seventeenth birthday.

Meanwhile we continued to live under increasing hardship. Jews were being expelled from parts of Bratislava and other parts of Slovakia. The local Judenrat decided that we would have to take in as many people as could reasonably exist under our roof. We had families in every room with their children. We also offered shelter to strangers who had nowhere else to go. A wig maker and her husband lived in one room. They knotted hair into wigs all day long, and I used to watch them as they continued to make wigs for orthodox Jewish women. The Freud brothers and their wives occupied another room. Aunt and Uncle Nachmias converted our dining room into their bedroom. Omama's apartment below us was also filled up with people. She gave refuge to Uncle David, Aunt Franziska and their two children Ruth and Marcel. Uncle Julius, Aunt Martha and Max also moved in after they had been evicted from their home. Later Aunt Selma and Uncle Bibi, along with their daughters Trude and Lilly, and sons Jossie and Robbie, joined us in the overcrowded house on Spitalska. However, despite having nearly all the family around us, we lived in constant fear. No one knew when the next round up would happen, or when the next knock on the door would wake us from our sleep. Since Judith's deportation an atmosphere of desperation and uncertainty engulfed us. It was shortly after this that my parents made the decision to escape Slovakia and flee to Hungary.

My parents established contact with grandmother Ilona in Sala as well as Aunts Serena and Nelly in Hungary. It was decided that my parents and I, Aunt Aranka, Uncle Jakob and their youngest and only remaining son, Thomas, would cross the border illegally and hide in Budapest. Their two other boys, my cousins Fritz and Erwin, went on the transport with Judith. They, like my parents, feared for their only remaining child. Maurice Friedlieb and his wife decided not to join us in the escape. Their daughter Erika went into hiding and survived. Later her parents were also deported and killed.

CHAPTER TWO

Hungary 1942-1943

UNCLE BIBI STERN was instrumental in finding us a reliable guide who was to be well rewarded when he agreed to take us across the border from Slovakia into Hungary. All preparations were done in the strictest secrecy. No one was allowed to talk. One day in late spring of 1942, we were ready. The weather was warm, but my mother made me put on more layers of garments. I tried to protest because it felt uncomfortable and I did not want to look fat! Mother won. Little did I realise that the clothes I left Bratislava in were the only clothes I was to have for the next year and a half. I wore several pairs of underpants, two jumpers and a new tweed woollen coat. It was beige with a removable hood and a beaver-fur collar. I wore comfortable leather boots and each of us carried an overnight bag. We did not go together to the railway station. My parents and I formed one group, and my Aunt Aranka, Uncle Jakob and Thomas formed another group. Each group was on their own. It would have been dangerous to be seen together – we would have been obvious and attracted attention. We had no documents. We left everything behind. We never mentioned any of our other possessions, nor did we grieve for them. We boarded the train in separate compartments and travelled to a remote village near the Hungarian border called Hegyeshalom.

The peasant guide, a middle-aged man, was waiting for us as arranged. He started to walk and we followed without a word spoken and my aunt, uncle and cousin were not far behind us. We were very careful not to attract attention. Slowly, it became dark. The sun had set behind the mountains and we reached what looked like the edge of a forest. We stopped. The guide approached us, gave us instructions and then collected his money. It was a very dangerous exercise as he could easily have walked away and abandoned us. But he was a good man; he kept his part of the bargain.

It was a clear night, no clouds and the moon was high in the sky, which spelt danger since it was too light. We had to rest and wait for the moon to sink. Eventually we started to walk. We were not allowed to talk and it seemed we walked for hours. We crossed a rivulet with water about ankle deep. I felt sorry for my new boots. We continued walking, the peasant guide always in the front. Sometimes he told us to duck. I was terribly scared and very tired but I did not dare complain or speak a word. Finally, he came to a halt. He told us that we had just crossed the border and that we would soon reach the end of the forest and arrive in a small village in Hungary. It was dawn.

At that point, another peasant took over and led us to a small cottage where we could rest. We were offered a room with a large bed. I remember the full feather pillows and white crisp starched linen and how good it was to go to sleep. Soon we were walking again. This time we had to reach the railway station and catch the train to Budapest. It was a difficult situation. In a small village people know one another very well and notice strangers. It would be so easy to attract unwanted attention. We saw many border guards with their funny feathered hats and their not-so-funny drawn bayonets.

We walked down to the station and boarded the train, which was waiting at the platform ready to depart. The guide purchased our tickets prior to our arrival and no further arrangements had to be made. We just had to be lucky not to be stopped and asked for documents of identification. Our luck held and a few hours later the train pulled into Keleti Station in Budapest. Keleti was big, old and grey and we were very much alone. Fortunately, we all spoke Hungarian which gave us an advantage.

Aunt Nelly from Szombathely had arranged a room in a boarding house on the Andrassy Körut near the centre of Budapest. It was an old and large apartment and the owners had let out all the rooms. We pretended to be from the country and were visiting Budapest because my father needed medical treatment. Since we had no documents, it was essential that we move out after three days, as we could not be registered. Grandmother Ilona in Sala prepared financial arrangements that were essential for us to survive.

A relative from Szombathely welcomed us to Budapest and handed my parents Hungarian money and coupons necessary to obtain food. It turned out that the coupons had been purchased on the black market. Another relative of my mother's, Julius Friedlieb, a distant cousin, was very helpful and managed to obtain for us everything we needed from the black market. Julius was a poor man who lived on the handouts he received from the family. My parents happily gave him as much money as they could in thanks for all his help.

As we could not stay in the Körut boarding house, my parents searched frantically for another suitable room. My father stayed indoors most of the time. He was petrified that one day he would be stopped on the streets and be arrested for lack of papers. Mother succeeded in finding another room for rent. It was in Wahrman Utca with a kind Jewish family, Mr and Mrs Willy König. We did not reveal our true identity to them. We always used the story that we were from the country and my father needed medical treatment in Budapest. We were farming people with our own food supply, so we didn't need coupons. There was, however, one problem with the room. The room was very small and it only had one double bed. There was hardly room for me. I slept on a stretcher bed on the floor.

After a short while, it was decided that I would have to move on and perhaps 'go back home to the country'. I was sent to Szombathely, where Aunt Nelly was to enjoy my company for a few weeks. Her brother-in-law, Louis Holzer, came to Budapest collected me, put me on a train and took me to Szombathely. At first I was happy, but soon I became very sad and lonely as I missed my parents very much. I was only sixteen years old and had never been away on my own before. Uncle Josef was not a friendly man. He was very well-to-do. The family lived in a beautiful house that had been built to their specifications. They had only one child, a daughter Aniko. She was very pretty but also very spoiled. No one except my aunt and uncle knew my real name. I had a false birth certificate and my false name was Rosie. I had to pretend I was visiting from the country. My Hungarian was not brilliant but somehow I managed with my limited vocabulary and got by. I slept on a sofa bed in the lounge room and cried throughout the nights when nobody saw me. My aunt was always kind and in a good mood, although I knew that her marriage was perhaps not a happy one. Aunt Nelly was a modern woman, a product of a Viennese boarding school. She loved music and sport. Aunt Nelly visited Bratislava many times before the war broke out and enjoyed being with her sisters. She guessed that I was unhappy and lonely and, after only a few weeks in Szombathely, I returned to Budapest.

When I returned, I broke down and could not stop crying and I begged my parents not to send me away again. They were still living in the room at the König family house and I found myself on the floor sleeping on the stretcher once again.

The König's invited my parents to join them one day for afternoon tea and to meet some friends of theirs. My parents accepted with pleasure but not without fear. During that evening, my parents had the most unusual encounter. The events of that night haunted my mother for the remainder of her life. As they sipped their tea and coffee, a man sitting across the table kept staring at my mother and after a while he asked if he could look at her hands. He took my mother's beautiful white hand and started to read her palm. He told her, 'Madam, I can see you are somehow troubled. I can also see that you had your left kidney attacked. I can see two children. Oh my God! One child is somewhere held in captivity, like in chains and she cannot move, only at the end of the war will she be free. But your other child is all right. She will move away after the war, very far away, crossing the sea to a land with lots of sunshine.' My mother pulled away her hand, excused herself and left the room. She was obviously very upset and disturbed and continued to be troubled by the man's words.

My cousin Rozsi and her husband Mano lived in Budapest after they were allowed to leave Vienna because they held Hungarian citizenship. Mano's hosiery factory in Vienna was closed and sealed for the duration of the war. During our stay in Budapest, Roszi was very supportive to us. We saw her often and she was glad to be with us. Her marriage was not good, but we knew little about her unhappiness. Roszi was strikingly beautiful. It soon became evident that she had an admiring boyfriend. Lajos Wertheimer was from Miskolc and he worshipped the ground Roszi walked on. His two sisters, Julie and Gizi, soon became our friends.

Gizi lived with her married sister, Julie and her husband and their two daughters. Their home was on Katona Joszef Street, not far from where we were living. Gizi was a dressmaker and my mother made arrangements for me to go to her salon in order to improve my sewing skills. My sewing soon became immaculate and I was of

great help to Gizi with the added benefit that she did not
have to pay me. I was just happy to spend the time where
I knew it was safe. However, it was also difficult because
they did not know my true identity and I had to be careful
and watch what I said or discussed. They might have had
some suspicions but they never asked any questions and
that was fine with me.

My parents were very keen to find new accommodation,
away from the König family. The room was too small and
under the cramped circumstances, my parents had no
privacy. Not far from the Königs, in fact just around the
corner from Wahrman Utca on Kresz Geza Utca, was a
block of newly completed apartments. Flats were offered
for rent. My parents went to enquire, found the place
suitable and rented a bachelor apartment on the fourth
floor. It looked nice and it was new and clean. It had a
small balcony, a small kitchenette and a bathroom. There
was also an elevator. We moved in and leased the most
important pieces of furniture. Grandmother Ilona sent
some feather pillows, quilts and linen as well as pots and
pans and crockery. We now had a household with only
the bare essentials. The cabinet sideboard was cleverly
designed. During the daytime it was decorative but at
night it miraculously transformed into a hidden double
bed for my parents. A comfortable mattress placed in a
corner was more than sufficient for me. I cleaned the
parquet floor until it was white and shiny. I scrubbed the
windowsills with turps and vinegar until I was satisfied
they were truly clean.

My father occupied himself with reading and making
his own cigarettes. He had a little device into which he

placed the fine paper, then the tobacco and, as he squeezed the machine together, out came uniform, perfect cigarettes. I often visited the library and brought books home to read. I was desperately trying to improve my Hungarian. Sometimes I went to the Gellert swimming pool around 6 am when the streets were not much frequented and I would not be seen by many people. I had no other entertainment nor was I allowed to go anywhere by myself. Sometimes my cousin Roszi took me to her attic apartment where I liked to help her with her cooking or housework. She then went with me to a cake shop where she bought vanilla slices that were delicious.

My father stayed between the four walls at home. Mother was courageous and went shopping although it was extremely dangerous as she had no documents at all. She also went to the Palestine office to enquire about permits or affidavits for us. But Miki Kraus, who was in charge of the office, was like a brick wall and never gave us any hope or encouragement.

Winter 1943 was fiercely cold. I had insufficient clothing though Aunt Nelly had sent me a beautiful Peshaniki fur coat that she did not wear any more. It fitted me perfectly. My mother lent me her brown leather handbag and also ordered lovely modern platform shoes for me. Those gorgeous platforms hardly ever left my feet. I finally left them in Auschwitz. We also went to the fashionable Vaci Utca and I was allowed to select and buy a lipstick-coloured woollen jumper. It was body hugging and I was very conscious and shy, as I did not wear a bra. My mother also bought some fabrics for herself as well as for me. Gizi made mother a nice tailored suit. I experimented on my own without supervision. The printed material turned into a dirndl and the gaberdine into a short-sleeved, double-breasted suit decorated with nice gold buttons.

Despite all these normal activities, the atmosphere in our home was usually tense. My parents were constantly worried and nervous. I do not know why, but one day my mother was very upset, and I was the one who copped it. I must have answered her back when I was not supposed to. This was really 'not on'. My mother lost her temper and hit me. That was the last time and I have not forgotten it. I was deeply hurt and did not talk to anyone for days.

In the world around us, the political situation worsened. Germany finally occupied Hungary after the Regent Admiral Horthy wavered in his allegiance to Hitler. And with the German army came the Gestapo and the agents of the 'Final Solution'. The spring and summer of 1944 marked the turn of Hungarian Jewry to feel the force of Nazi anti-semitism. Within weeks of the occupation, Eichmann and his henchmen – many of them Hungarian Nazis – had the trains rolling to Auschwitz.

Suddenly, those people who were in hiding were denounced. Caretakers in apartment houses were now appointed as spies and were paid by KEOK (Police Department to Catch Foreign Jewish Fugitives), when they denounced 'illegal' Jews. Our 'concierge' was a very special person who fortunately didn't ask too many questions. The streets in the city were now full of denouncers. My father was once recognised by an old friend from Bratislava who now worked with the KEOK police. He approached my father and told him: 'Disappear quickly. If anyone sees you talking to me, they will arrest you.' People who were denounced in the street were deported to Auschwitz. Throughout the summer of 1944 the roundups continued and we lost contact with Grandmother Ilona and the family in Sala. Then we heard no more from our family in Ballasagyarmat and Szombathely. They were all arrested, deported and murdered in Auschwitz. For Jews in Budapest there was a calm before the storm as the first deportations began with rural Jewish communities. Budapest would be the last major centre for round ups.

Daily routines became a torture. If I had to venture on to the street, I had to be particularly careful. There were denouncers or 'watchers' throughout Budapest who were paid by KEOK to hunt Jews. We avoided crowds in case someone recognised us as had happened to my father. We were always nervous and scared that any movement on our part might attract attention and give us away. We heard that people who were arrested were 'sent to Poland' or 'sent to Auschwitz'. And while I didn't fully understand what that meant, it was enough to send shivers down my spine. Inside the apartment, we were always listening for strange sounds that could signal a raid. We couldn't have conversations with other residents in case we let something 'slip' accidentally as to our true identity. Life was so tense, I don't know how we endured it.

By early 1944 there were air raids almost daily. The sirens had the most frightful sound and gave me chills every time I heard them. Everyone had to go down to the air shelters. It created great difficulties for us. We did not want to go down four flights of stairs and register our names. We never knew if someone would recognise us. One never knew what questions would be asked. We met all the tenants in the air shelter. Sometimes we sat there for long hours before the all-clear sirens sounded to let us return to our apartments. One elderly couple, Mr and Mrs Fried, and their daughter were also among the tenants. They were fugitives from Yugoslavia, hiding like us in one of the apartments. I met their daughter Fritzi in Bergen-Belsen after the Liberation and she told me about their nightmares in Budapest.

Raids or *razzias* were conducted during the daytime and often at night. Roadblocks were very frightening and dangerous. The KEOK police looked for Jews who were hiding. They would block off the streets and then house searches took place. We were in our apartment most of the time and thought ourselves to be relatively safe, at least for the time being. One day we were suddenly warned by our caretaker that the street would be blocked off from both ends and that a house to house search would take place within a few minutes. They told us that we had enough time to leave the place, just to take our handbags and to walk out. They also assured us that they themselves would not denounce us and confessed to us that they were Communists. They also told us that they suspected we were hiding illegal fugitives and we were in danger. We were grateful for the warning, but at the same time we were also desperate. We left the place immediately and never returned. We arranged for the furniture to be returned to where we had leased it.

My mother took my father to the Jewish Hospital where one of the nursing sisters was the daughter of an old friend. Father pretended to be very sick and the nurse tucked him into a bed to protect him. My mother and I were now on the streets. We walked for hours during the day and rented any room that was available. The rooms were in derelict areas. I often slept in a chair as bugs invaded the beds the very minute they smelt human blood to be sucked. I hated it! I just could not tolerate it. Sometimes we could not find a room to rent and when night-time closed in, we would look for any hiding place for just a few hours. I was unhappy and very scared. We sought shelter wherever we could find it, under rooftops or as happened one night, under an ironing table in a laundry. The sirens went off and we could not go to an air-raid shelter. Mother held me tight while the entire building shook with the sound of the heavy bombers flying over head. This was on the top floor of an apartment block and the bombers were literally flying over our heads. I was so scared I sobbed throughout the rest of the night. It was an impossible situation. We were like hunted animals and, like a hunted animal, we grew more and more desperate and panic-stricken with every day.

CHAPTER THREE

~~⟨∾⟩~~

Return to Bratislava: Spring 1944

My FATHER WAS relatively safe in the hospital and this gave him the opportunity to contact people in Bratislava and make provisions for our return into Slovakia. The situation in Hungary was worsening every day. We simply had no idea how long we could keep running and hiding. Bratislava was home and it was familiar. My parents believed it would be better for us to return home. Aunt Aranka and Uncle Jakob agreed, and they, with their son Thomas, prepared to join us. At least we would be among people we knew and trusted. We contacted Julius Friedlieb, mother's cousin, to let him know we had to leave Kresz Geza immediately. He also acted as our courier. He was a good man.

It was early spring 1944. The return trip was tense though uneventful. Julius established the contacts with my father and the same man who acted as our guide a year before was re-employed for the same amount of money. I wore my gaberdine suit with the gold buttons, and underneath I had my floral dirndl and the pink jumper. I wore my platform shoes. Everything else was left behind. I did not even think of my inherited fur coat.

Father looked worried. He had lost a lot of weight, but he remained strong and encouraged all of us, never stopping to think about himself. He was a remarkable man and I loved him very much. On the day of our departure, we set out for Keleti station and boarded the train to the little border village we had visited in the previous year. As before, both groups travelled separately. After a few hours the Budapest train arrived in the village. We disembarked and started to walk towards the village and then towards the border. My mother wore a scarf over her head imitating most of the local women. I did the same, although I protested vigorously: I didn't want to look like a peasant!

At nearly seventeen, I was concerned with how I looked. I had grown a lot in Hungary and was no longer a little girl. The Budapest fashions greatly impressed me (especially that women did not wear a bra), although I don't know if they had the same effect on my mother! Though I thought I was a woman, I was still only a child, and had not absorbed the full seriousness of the events taking place. Being fashionable while trying to escape made you stand out. It was the worst thing to do. I knew we were in danger because we were Jews, but I still couldn't imagine people would actually do us harm.

My father pretended to be sick and had a blanket covering him. Mother helped him to walk and I pretended to be as assured as I could and just kept walking. The Hungarian gendarmes were on the platform of the station checking papers and travel documents. Of course we had neither. We prayed silently that we would get through.

My parents and I were not stopped, but Aunt Aranka and Uncle Jakob were. Fifteen-year-old Thomas kept walking and was not challenged. My aunt and uncle were arrested then and there and taken away. Their son followed us and we kept walking away. There was no looking back. My aunt and uncle vanished, deported to Auschwitz. We never saw them again. Thomas never spoke about his parents. He buried his sadness deep within.

We met our guide as arranged and he led us out of the village until we reached the forest. We encountered ankle-deep water once again as we waded through the same streams and swamplands that we crossed in 1942. We walked through the night and eventually crossed the border into Slovakia. We managed to board a train for Bratislava and arrived home at Spitalska 45, exhausted physically and mentally.

The house was still there with many members of the Rosenberger family, and of course the painful memories of those who had been deported about whom we still knew nothing.

Our home looked the same from the outside but inside it was a different matter. Furniture was shoved up against the walls making the rooms look like storerooms, which is what they had really become, except the 'stores' were human beings crowded together and frightened. We tried to find some of our belongings that we had entrusted to different friends before we fled to Budapest. However, there was not much to find. I did find my *Bat Mitzvah* bicycle alongside Judith's. Both bicycles became very important for the family. With them we could go and buy food from nearby country villages. My father and I did exactly that. It was dangerous to leave the city, but we had to eat. My father and I pedalled out to surrounding villages where he had friends and we were able to get food. I was more than happy to be out riding with him. The excursions were long and tiring but I did not mind and rather looked forward to the next expedition. If all this sounds a little 'romantic', I must say that being out in the open countryside riding a bicycle with my father was much better than being cooped up in the house with people who were struggling with fear and anxiety. Most importantly, we had to eat.

I looked up some of my old friends and contacted Gerti Schweiger who now lived with her widowed mother in an old derelict part of Bratislava. They had been evicted from their former home. Another friend, Greta Fischer who was about the same age as me, had joined the partisans and I was unable to contact her. Other friends had either disappeared or gone into hiding.

Although life was hard, it was not impossible, as it had become in Hungary. We were still together as a family. We were still in our home and we could still move about, although we did have to be extremely careful not to attract the attention of the Nazi Hlinka guards who enjoyed beating Jews. Deportations had slowed in 1942 and it seemed Slovakian Jews were safe for a short time. Of course the word 'safe' means one thing to someone who has nothing to fear, and quite another to someone who worries whether their loved ones will come home at night. Early in 1944, transports started rolling out of

Hungary for Auschwitz. By comparison, Slovakia was quiet for the time being – a very short time indeed.

Another cousin, Eugene (the son of my Aunt Frieda and Uncle Oskar), was a young solicitor who worked with the underground and had contacts with the Americans. Slovakia was technically an independent country and had foreign embassies in Bratislava, including the United States legation. Eugene was able to provide all members of the family with skillfully produced false papers that stated we were American citizens, and therefore subject to the protection of the United States. These documents should have protected us from the Slovakian police, the Hlinka guards, and even the Germans present in Slovakia were obliged under Slovakian and international law to respect 'protected nationals'.

However, conditions in Slovakia took a dangerous turn in late August 1944. An uprising against the Tiso regime broke out in Central and Eastern Slovakia and the Germans used this as the excuse to invade and occupy the country under the pretext of assisting the Slovakian government combat partisans. German troops marched into Slovakia and as always the Gestapo and SS were not far behind. Our lives were now ruled by terror.

Sometime after the war, I learnt about the fate of my cousin Eugene. For those who wanted to, money was to be made in denouncing Jews. The Germans paid a bounty to anyone who revealed the whereabouts of Jews in hiding. Shortly after the Germans marched in, news came that deportations were to resume. Eugene was denounced to the Hlinka Guard and the SS. German agents who wanted to discover other Jews in hiding followed him. One day, while walking in the city, Eugene must have realised he was being followed. He started to run and entered the first house that offered some protection. SS guards chased him into the house and caught him on the third floor. From there the SS threw my cousin out the window. He died instantly. This was another open murder of a member of my family. It was a great blow. What else were the Germans capable of?

My parents were convinced that even with the 'American' papers we had no choice but to go into hiding. Our next door neighbours, the Chmelar family, had been friends of my parents for many years and my parents trusted them completely. Both husband and wife were pharmacists, as well as being devout Roman Catholics. They owned two apartments. One was behind the pharmacy in the building next to ours and the other was in a nearby modern building called 'The Avion'. The Chmelar's accepted a few items for safekeeping when we left for Hungary in 1942. Now they offered us the Avion apartment as a hiding place. We accepted and moved in. Thomas came with us – he had no one else now. We took only the essentials – no luxuries. Our cold and dry foodstuffs formed our new diets. During the day, we stayed indoors for most of the time. We were desperate not to give ourselves away through talking or moving about, nor could we even flush the toilet before evening. Mrs Chmelar supplied us with some food that she brought with her at night when she returned from the pharmacy. This was our only contact with the outside world. During the day, from behind drawn curtains, I stood and watched the traffic and counted people walking on the footpath.

Mrs Chmelar had one son who lived with his parents. He never spoke to us and I felt he resented us being there. He was a university student and probably disagreed with his parent's views and actions. It was known that anyone found sheltering Jews placed their lives and those of their families in great danger. Difficult as it was, we managed to stay in contact with the rest of the family, especially the Bardos and Friedlieb families. They had an arrangement to warn each other if they knew danger of a round up of Jews. The signal would be a telephone call with the message 'Let us go to the market'. This meant 'Go into hiding now!'. We had been in the Chmelar apartment for two weeks when we were denounced.

CHAPTER FOUR

Sered: Autumn 1944

ONE AFTERNOON IN early August 1944, we heard the key turning in the door. Everyone froze. It was highly unusual for Mrs Chmelar to come home during the day. Something had to be wrong. My mother looked as though she was about to die. The door opened and Mrs Chmelar stood there with the greengrocer who was a tenant in one of the shops owned by my family. He stood beside Mrs Chmelar in the uniform of the Slovakian fascists complete with brown shirt and swastika armband. Nobody moved. They were both quite friendly and told us not to be alarmed, as we were 'American citizens'. We would be safe and protected. I didn't believe either of them. The grocer's smile was so false. I knew the truth. He was a collaborator and may have pressured Mrs Chmelar into abandoning us. Mrs Chmelar told us it was advisable for us to leave her apartment and join other 'foreign' nationals in Marianka (Marienthal), a small hamlet not far from Bratislava. American citizens were supposedly offered protection for the duration of the war, which didn't appear to make too much sense, since by October 1944 the United States had been at war with Germany for nearly two years. I do not think anyone believed their story but we had no option. We packed our belongings into our overnight bags and went with the grocer.

I cannot remember clearly but I think it was the grocer who drove us to Marianka in his delivery truck. There, an old baroque style castle stood majestically in the middle of a beautifully groomed park. When we arrived, the castle appeared deserted, but we quickly found other 'Americans' already present. The grocer made several 'deliveries' bringing the rest of the family, including Omama, to Marianka. During this time, the weather was mild and we slept on the floors of the rooms we were placed in. Now we could only wait to see what would happen. Everyone was anxious and fearful, but no one spoke since we were afraid of more betrayals. We trusted no one. About two weeks later the tension broke. At that time, we were made quite aware that we no longer had any control over our fate.

One morning around the end of August or early September, we heard a commotion outside in the grounds of the castle. SS guards and Hlinka forces surrounded the building. A high ranking SS officer rode into the park on a horse. I later discovered that this man was the notorious Jew-hater, *SS Hauptsturmführer* Alois Brunner, Eichmann's henchman. Brunner had been sent by Eichmann into Slovakia to finish the deportations and make the place *Judenrein* – 'free of Jews'. Brunner was a cruel and sadistic man who enjoyed making defenceless people suffer. All we knew at the time was that this SS officer had us firmly under his control.

We were ordered to dress and come out of our rooms, one at a time in single file. My parents were outside already, and then it was my turn. As I walked through the door, I found myself directly in front of Brunner who sat high on his horse and held a gun aimed directly at me. He was looking at me, although I have no idea what was going through his mind. His face was stern and showed no trace of human feeling. As far as he was concerned, I was less than a sick dog. I couldn't think, and I must have stopped walking, so great was the shock. I was sure he was going to shoot me. A guard must have yelled something at me, because I started walking again, moving over to my parents, Thomas and other members of the family. When I reached them I was so frightened my body was shaking all over.

Once the castle was emptied and all the detainees were lined up, we were ordered to start marching. Armed guards marched alongside us. Mr Haar and his daughter Hilda were brave and made a desperate move. As we marched away from the castle onto the highway, they darted into the hedges that bordered the road and disappeared. I was certain one of the Hlinka guards saw them escape, but he chose not to do anything. Not long after this, another Hlinka guard came up to me and whispered, 'Step out carefully and come with me. I will help you.' I looked at him with surprise and reacted by thanking him and told him that I would accept if my parents could join me. He refused and I marched on.

A little further along the road we came to a railway siding where a train with cattle cars attached was waiting for us. We were herded into the cattle trucks, sealed inside and carted off to Sered. No one told us anything. Among ourselves, we wondered where we were going, but no one knew for certain. The Nazis used this fear of not knowing as a clever way of keeping us under control. We were usually so frightened and scared that resistance was hardly possible. The train did not travel far and we reached our new destination shortly. It was the transit camp Sered, although we did not know it was only a temporary stop.

Sered is about 55 kilometres north-east of Bratislava on the river Vah. It was one of the main collection points for Slovakian Jews in the final roundups after the failed uprising.* From here, the transports were sent to Auschwitz. The camp served a double purpose. First, it was a transit camp and most of the population stayed for brief periods before being sent on the trains for Auschwitz. Secondly, Sered was also a labour camp for a small population of prisoners who were kept busy working in factories. Most of them were cabinetmakers who made furniture for the Hlinka guards as well as for the offices of Eichmann and Brunner. Only a very few of these artisans managed to avoid deportation and survive.

After we were taken from the train, we were put into the camp. We were ushered into huts, huge dormitories with bunks on each side of the wall and also down the centre. While the dormitories were very orderly and relatively clean, they were also terribly crowded. During our internment in the camp more and more people were shoved in until conditions became nearly unbearable. Clearly the Germans were planning something else for

---

*See page 143

us. My parents shared one bunk, while I slept on the floor. I was used to it by now. My mother had a small feather pillow covered with a pale pink damask pillowslip. I can almost see her dark hair and flawless white face resting on it. To our surprise, we found Mr Haar and Hilda in the transit camp with us. Their escape attempt had failed and they had been caught and sent back to join the rest of us.

We were now prisoners with no control over our lives. Roll call was a trial. We would stand outside our barrack and wait to be counted. Brunner often came to watch – he found it amusing. He enjoyed the fact that he had total mastery over us. And he demonstrated his contempt for us at every opportunity. Sitting on his horse, Brunner would entertain himself by shooting prisoners at random. He was an excellent sharpshooter. On the day before we arrived in Sered, old Mr Grossmann was sweeping the courtyard. Brunner rode by, saw the old man and shot him dead. In his perverted manner, he appointed Mr Grossmann's son, Hugo, as a camp policeman. I met Hugo shortly after his 'appointment'. He was a tall, handsome young man and with his police cap and armband he looked quite impressive. We became friends and to make our stay more bearable, he sometimes brought extra bread for us. This kindness made a big difference for us. Food was always in short supply and we were nearly always hungry. The approaching winter made us even more anxious about our futures, so every scrap of food helped.

About ten days after we arrived in Sered, we were ordered to get our hand luggage and line up outside our barrack. It was now early to mid-September 1944. We were given a food ration – a single slice of bread a bit bigger than the regular piece. More orders were shouted at us and then we were marched to the railway siding which was next to an old abandoned factory. Our train consisted of the locomotive engine and many cattle cars that were all marked with special numbers. We had to be registered and then wait until our name was called out. All the time, we were pushed and shoved, yelled at and abused by the guards. And then I was shoved into a car along with my parents. There were about 120 people crammed into a cattle truck that normally would have held eight horses or forty adults. Just before the door was slammed shut, Hugo Grossmann ran over and passed a small paper-wrapped parcel to me. It was a piece of roast duck. Not much was said, but my eyes and his were not dry. He promised me he would look me up once the war was over. Then the doors were rolled shut and bolted.

Mother and I ate the duck. I remember that it tasted delicious. Father declined since he still kept the laws of *Kashrut* even in circumstances like these. Now the cattle car was sealed we were in the dark. Surrounded by scared and panicky people, we could hardly sit or lie down. Around us, I could hear voices sobbing, others prayed and others moaned quietly. These were the sounds of a terrible desolate pain from deep in the human heart. Mothers nursed babies, and some older people even suffered heart attacks. People lost control of their bowels and soon the car was filled with the stench of human excrement, most of which did not end up in the single bucket provided for our sanitary needs. I refused to use the bucket for two days, but finally I had no choice. I begged my mother to cover me with a blanket while I used the bucket; the feeling of humiliation was so intense. All the manners and customs I had grown up with were being stripped away from me.

How long we were on that train I cannot remember. Time meant nothing to me anymore. In the dark, on this terrible train journey, day and night blended, and all the time we were hungry and desperately thirsty Our only consolation was that we were together as a family. Omama was with her beloved children and family, and to us she was a tower of strength. Not a word of complaint or lament passed her lips: her courage helped us all. Our destination was the subject of much speculation. The word 'Auschwitz' was heard, but it meant very little to us at the time. All we knew was that we were passing through towns and junctions, with occasional views of mountains – the Carpathians. We were heading north towards Poland. The train often stopped to allow military transports priority, and to change guards' shifts and bring on food – not that we prisoners saw any of it. On this trip food was only for the Germans and their collaborators and their dogs.

After a long and seemingly unending journey, the train slowed and came to a halt. We had arrived. I could hear dogs barking and voices shouting in German. All of a sudden, the bolts on our doors were slammed back and the door rolled open. Daylight flooded into our dark car and the light hit our eyes and blinded us. Strangely, amidst all the yelling and screaming I could hear music. An orchestra was playing light operatic tunes to 'welcome' us. It hit me that the music belonged not to the world of the living, but of the dead. The merry tunes were really the songs of unbelievable heartache and immeasurable sorrow. The bizarre nature of everything I saw and heard stunned me. All around people were being pulled out of the cars. Guards shouted at them – *Raus, raus!* Strange figures in blue and grey striped garb with caps ran around telling us to leave our baggage on the ramp. And all the time everything had to be done in a hurry – *Schnell, schnell!* I looked up and saw an iron gate over which there was an inscription: *Arbeit macht Frei* – Freedom through Work. I had arrived in Auschwitz.

CHAPTER FIVE

Konzentrationslager Auschwitz-Birkenau

AUSCHWITZ WAS A bewildering and strange environment. At first, I didn't know why I had to hurry up. I did not understand the meaning of *Arbeit macht Frei*. I didn't even understand that we had arrived in Auschwitz, or its terrible history. I was not aware of the awful fate that awaited me. We dropped our luggage on the ramp and saw how the prisoners in striped clothing came to pick up all our baggage. They took it all and loaded it onto lorries.

I learnt later that these prisoners were known as *Kanadians. Kanada* was the nickname given to the thirty-five or so warehouses packed with the stolen and looted possession of Jews from all over Europe. Everything was stashed into *Kanada* – clothes, spectacles, women's hair, artificial limbs, valises, shoes, even toothbrushes – anything that the Germans could use. We, the 'useful' living, were destined to be used by German industry to keep the Third Reich going a little longer. Companies such as Buna, I.G. Farben, Siemens, Thiessen and Höchst, grew fat on Jewish slave labour, and on my labour as well.

From the ramp by the train, I could see the camp. I know now that I was looking at one section of the Auschwitz camps, Birkenau. The original camp was about two kilometres away, and the third section, Buna-Monowitz, was a huge factory site, further away again. What I saw was a vast beehive, a jungle of filthy dog houses. It was like a cage to trap living Jews. We were ordered to separate, women to one side, men to the other. Women with children, the elderly, infirm and ill people were sent to yet another line. Everyone was to be looked after, we were told. The shouts and cries were deafening as panicking families were ripped apart. We were tired; we were hungry and thirsty; we did as we were told. We obeyed like zombies. I was in a line with my mother waiting for whatever would happen next.

I looked over towards the ramp and saw women prisoners well dressed in leather jackets and leather boots. They had armbands with the word KAPO printed on them. I saw one of them using a whip on the new arrivals urging them to hurry up. I stopped breathing. It was a girl I knew, Eta, who had been in the same class as Judith and had been on that first transport with my sister in March 1942. I was disgusted at what I saw, and yelled out, 'Eta! What are you doing?' Hearing her name, she stopped, turned around, looked at me and recognised me before saying, 'Olly, believe me I am not human anymore. I am an animal.' I did not see Eta again in Auschwitz, but met her many months later in Bergen-Belsen. Nearby, I saw another woman I knew, Mrs Fischer from Bratislava. She had been a restaurant owner before the war.

Mrs Fischer recognised my mother and came over to us. 'Mrs Rosenberger,' she whispered to my mother. 'Listen carefully and remember what I say. Never volunteer for anything!' Then she produced a small piece of carrot and gave it to my mother saying, 'And remember this is a piece of gold.'

Still in the line, I saw other women and men prisoners, shabby and terribly thin pushing or pulling two-wheeled carts. Every now and again they stopped and picked up what looked to be piles of rubbish from the ground. Some of the carts were heavy with big loads. Of course the 'rubbish' was the bodies of the dead, and the carts were heading towards the crematoria. In the distance I saw chimneys. Dark grey smoke with streaks of purple escaped wide openings at the top. At that stage, I did not know what they were. The smell in the camp was rotten and putrid and poisoned the air.

Waiting on the ramp were many SS men, all dressed in their immaculate black uniforms and highly polished boots. One of the SS sat behind a table. He was a good-looking young man, pink-cheeked and well groomed. I remember that his boots were particularly well kept and he wore leather gloves. Shortly after, I learned this handsome man was also a cruel sadist who performed hideous experiments on children and other prisoners. He was Dr Josef Mengele, the 'Angel of Death'. With other tired and bewildered women I stood in the queue. Immediately behind me were my Aunt Franziska and her daughter Ruth. Father stood with Omama and his sisters and their children giving them his support. Suddenly they were led away. There was no time to say anything, no goodbyes. It all happened so fast. They were gone.

As we drew near to the table where Mengele sat, we were ordered to strip completely and drop any luggage we were still carrying. What? Strip naked in the open in front of one another, and in front of all the SS men? There was no choice. We did as we were ordered and took all our clothes off. The SS men leered at us with vicious and curious stares. Now we were told to form a single line and to walk towards Mengele who looked us up and down deciding who was fit, young and healthy enough to be sent to the right. Anyone who was not considered good enough, too young or too old, over-weight, perhaps with scarring or something else that did not please Mengele was sent to the left. We soon realised that the right side meant something better than the left. I approached the table. Mengele looked me up and down like a butcher inspecting meat and waved me to the right where I joined the others who had been 'saved'. My mother endured the same 'inspection' and was sent to the right as well. I was seventeen and mother thirty-nine and we had passed the first *Selektion* in Auschwitz.

Ruth, who was sixteen, was sent over to our side and then Aunt Franziska stood before Mengele. An abdominal operation had left her with a scar and Mengele pointed to the left. Ruth immediately walked back to the table and stood in front of Mengele and pleaded for her mother: 'Please let my mother be with me.' Mengele stood up grabbed Ruth and slapped her hard across the face, before shoving Aunt Franzi to the right. It seemed a miracle! Ruth had saved her mother. Both women survived the war as well as Uncle David and Marcel.

When *Selektion* was finished and Mengele had decided our fates, the column on the left moved in one direction, and we on the right were marched to a large hall not far from the railway siding. Again, the guards ordered us into lines. This time I was to be shaven. All the time Kapos yelled orders at us, and beat those who didn't move quickly enough. The shaving was even more humiliating than standing naked before Mengele. We were told that we would be deloused and shaven. I wondered, 'Why should I be deloused? We are clean, civilised and cultured people!'

Inmates did the delousing and shaving. The Germans had very little direct contact with us. Those in charge of this operation were privileged prisoners who had probably been in Auschwitz a long time. Conversation among them was mostly in Polish, but I also heard Slovakian and German. Naked, I waited with my mother, aunt and cousin for our turn. The woman who shaved me had a sarcastic grin on her face. She took the blunt clippers and cut off my curly shoulder-length hair. I then had to lift up my arms and my armpits were shaven, and then my pubic hair. The clippers were so blunt that I bled from the shaven areas. Next, I had to stand before a prisoner holding a bucket full of horrible smelling carbolic liquid. Using a makeshift mop, a stick with strips of rags hanging from the end, the prisoner dipped the mop into the bucket and then smeared it over my shaven head, under my arms and between my legs. My bald and broken skin stung from the contact with that horrible substance. Now that I was sanitised, disinfected and deloused, I went to look for my mother.

I called out her name and when this figure in front of me responded, I didn't recognise her, even though she had been beside me the whole time. My mother once had the most beautiful thick, dark black hair. Now she was bald. It was a terrible sight. Oddly, it was almost funny and in my anxiety, I started to laugh. It was a tragic comedy, or a comic tragedy?

Ordered into yet another queue, we lined up to receive our clothes. In front of us was a pile of old rags. A woman prisoner in charge handled the distribution. There was no time to find a dress to fit, and I took what was thrown at me. I was given a black dress, completely torn though perhaps it could have been pretty once. It had a small white pattern in the fabric. Now this ragged dress had to cover my naked body. There was no underwear and I was given two different shoes – one flat-heeled that was too small and one high-heeled that was too large. Later on, the shoes were replaced with wooden clogs that were too big for me. However, without footwear in Auschwitz, my life expectancy would have been very short. My mother went through a similar dilemma with her 'clothes'.

The next stage of our initiation was numbering. A prisoner painted a number across my back and over my left breast. Many prisoners later received tattoos, some on the outside of their arms, others on the inside. Although I was an inmate of Auschwitz, I was not tattooed. Thousands of people arrived every day and there was not enough time to process every prisoner. Very young prisoners did not get their number tattooed since they might not have 'lasted' too much longer and the Germans considered this a waste of ink. It was possible that I was one of those 'young ones' upon whom it was not worth wasting ink.

Our induction and registration complete, we were marched to the barracks. I can't remember exactly but I believe I was in the 'B Lager'. The barracks were long, hangar-like buildings, close to one another, in many rows. Many of them looked as though they were made of old sheets of corrugated iron and mended with sheets of cardboard. 'Dog kennels' would have been a better description than 'barrack'. Inside, there were bunks on either side, made of wood and three tiers high covered with bits of dirty straw. Four women shared one narrow uncomfortable bunk, making it impossible to get a decent night's sleep or rest. Along the centre, between the two rows of bunks, was an elevated platform that ran the length of the barrack. It was built from red bricks, neatly tuckpointed with white paint. I have no idea what this platform represented or what it was supposed to be used for. I only saw the Kapos and the *Stubovas* (or *Stubenälteste*) standing on it when they were yelling their orders to us.

Many of us suffered from intestinal problems caused by the so-called 'diet'. This resulted in the latrines smelling unbelievably foul. The latrine block was separate from the other barracks. It was a flat, long wooden seat with holes punctured all the way along. The smell in the latrine was so bad I nearly vomited the first time I had to use it. But there was no option – I had to use it. Of course, many inmates grew too weak to struggle to the latrines and soiled themselves in the bunks.

These degrading situations were all a part of the dehumanisation plan of the Nazis.

Near the entrance to the barrack was a small room with a bunk covered with a blanket. This was the 'private room' of our *Stubova*. She was in charge of the inmates in our barrack. Twice a day, in the morning at 4am and in the afternoon at 5pm, the *Stubova* would start shouting and ordering us out of the barrack. This procedure was followed by rollcall and was dreaded by every inmate. Outside the barrack the 'streets' of the Lager were rough, dirty, pot-holed and puddled with contaminated swamp water. We had to stand motionless until the SS were satisfied with the counting. Sometimes, people collapsed with exhaustion, but the roll had to be taken. Even the dead were dragged out so that the numbers tallied.

Once the SS were satisfied that we were all accounted for, the distribution of the food ration took place. In the morning, we received a small tin mug filled with *Ersatzkaffee* (a substitute coffee made from chicory), which was really black water, and a small slice of black military bread. At night, we were given a dish of soup. This so-called soup was more like warm water. Sometimes we found sand, pebbles or grass in it, but if we were lucky there was a peel of turnip or a piece of potato. The soup was brought to the front of the barracks in large drums. When queuing for the soup, it was essential to find the right place in the line. If one hurried and wanted to be among the first, all you got was a bowl of murky hot water. If you were too slow and were at the end of the line, there might not be anything left at all, and so you would go hungry. The best place was the centre of the line. Enough soup would be left in the drum and it was still warm and thick. You might even have a chance of getting something solid in the soup. I learnt these tricks quickly. It was a matter of life and death.

It was not until after the war that I learnt that the food was possibly poisoned. The 'coffee' and soup were laced with bromide. Bromide stopped menstruation in women, which was in reality a blessing since we had no sanitary measures anyway. Our systems were badly affected nonetheless and most of us did not function normally for many years after Liberation. This also happened to me.

While I was in Auschwitz-Birkenau, I was not selected for work, nor was my mother. Neither were we tattooed. Thousands of people were still arriving in the camp. There was probably no time. 'Processing' the new arrivals took precedence over everything else. The gas chambers and crematoria were engaged day and night. It was still fairly warm even though it was autumn, but the coming winter was to be one of the coldest in recent European history. As the days rolled by, I became like my fellow prisoners, lethargic and generally disinterested. When someone remarked that it was 'Rosh Hashanah' or 'Yom Kippur', the Jewish High Holy Days, we did not react. Emotions had died within us. If they didn't, it would have been too much. The pain from what was happening to us would have been too much to bear. No, it was better not to let yourself feel anything, just stay alive for another day.

Auschwitz had some non-Jewish prisoners as well. The Nazis used a coloured triangle system to mark out different categories. Jews wore yellow; political prisoners, red; homosexuals, pink; Jehovahs Witnesses, purple; criminals, green; prostitutes and 'asocials', black; emigres, blue; and Gypsies, brown. Many of the Gypsies were Kapos and some were known for their cruelty and anti-semitic outbursts.

The weather quickly cooled and the nights were freezing. Our rags were not sufficient to warm our poor disfigured bodies. I felt the cold on my shaven head and my feet were blistered and sore. My raw gums bled and hurt all the time.

These were minor problems compared with the terror that went through the barracks every time the SS appeared. On a daily basis, a number of SS men entered the barrack and forcefully collected about twenty young women who never returned. They were taken to Mengele's laboratory where he performed obscene experiments upon them. This 'genius' of a doctor specialised his skill on twins in order to try to understand something of the genetics of inheritance. He also injected blue dye into the eyes of dark-eyed Gypsy children and watched the effect on his young subjects. Mengele was determined to find a way to create blue-eyed, blond-haired and fair-skinned Aryans for his Führer. An entertainment devised by Mengele was to invite SS sharpshooters into the laboratory and invite them to shoot the nipples off his 'patients'. Most of his 'subjects' died excruciating deaths.

Sometimes the SS changed their tactics and offered a glass of milk to anyone who volunteered. There would always be someone for whom the pangs of hunger was too much, and they would offer themselves. My mother would cover me with her body every time the SS entered the barracks. At seventeen, I would have been eligible for Mengele's attentions. I was never spotted and was therefore spared. Mrs Fischer's earlier advice rang loud in our minds.

After many weeks in Auschwitz-Birkenau, living in mind-numbing fear and constant danger, there was a sudden change. After morning roll call one day, we were told not to return to the barrack. Chills ran down my spine. We did not know what to expect, but we were certain it would be bad. We were marched into an open space in one of the Lager streets. Here we had to line up and await *Selektion*. Mengele arrived, 'inspected' us and selected most of our group for hard labour. We waited for further orders, and remained standing for the rest of the day. Evening came and we were still standing in the yard. We stood for what seemed like days. Occasionally other bald, shabbily clad and sad creatures were sent to join us. We were not fed. Many collapsed and fell to the ground where they lay scattered unaided. I fell asleep cradled in my mother's lap. And still we waited.

I was wakened to the familiar sound of shouting. SS men and SS women along with the Kapos ordered us into lines, counted us and then marched us off. At this point, I didn't care anymore. They could do what they liked. I just walked with the rest of the group, with my mother beside me. I saw the high wire fences and knew that they were charged with high voltage electricity. Very few people committed suicide by touching the wire. I only remember seeing one woman's body hanging limp and dead on the wire. We arrived at a ramp outside the Lager fence. Waiting for us was an old locomotive and the familiar sight of the cattle trucks. We formed a small transport so there were only a few cars. The locomotive was puffing steadily and was waiting to move as soon as its human cargo was loaded. Each of us was given a slice of bread and a tiny square of margarine. Loaded onboard and sealed in our cars, we felt the train move as it started to huff and puff, jerking forward and throwing us from side to side. We were tired, and physically and mentally exhausted. Miraculously our spirits were not entirely broken. Though we had no idea where the train was taking us, we didn't really care as long as it was away from Auschwitz.

We passed through towns and villages, the names of which I cannot recall. However, I was aware that we had left Poland and that we were somewhere in Germany. Eventually the train stopped. We were ordered to get out and line up again. The columns had to be orderly and the lines straight. We were counted. There were about 1000 women prisoners from Auschwitz-Birkenau in groups of 100. We were all standing on a German railway station. It was cold in the dawn of an early winter day. I had survived Auschwitz. On a small railway station building I could see the name of the place. I had arrived at a place called Trachenberg in late October of 1944.

CHAPTER SIX

Kurzbach

SURROUNDED BY HEAVILY armed SS guards we were ordered to march towards the city where we would go to a *Brausebad* – a bathhouse – for a shower. It could not have been a worse announcement. We were panic-stricken. 'Bathhouse' was, of course, the Nazi term for 'gas chamber'. Now in this new place, we were certain that we would be taken and gassed. We could not speak; we had to obey. It was an unbelievable surprise to discover when we arrived, that the grey, old building in front of us, was in fact, a bathhouse.

We entered a large hall. We saw a tiled floor and showerheads neatly in a row suspended from old rusty pipes. This sight gave us the 'secure feeling' that it was a real bathhouse and not some German trick. We stripped off our flimsy torn rags from our bodies and were shown to a place under a showerhead. Then we waited. Suddenly we felt water! For the moment, we indulged in the luxury of real warm water though it would also be the last time I would see running water for a long time to come. I was able to wash myself and for the first time in months, I actually felt a little bit more human. Before we were allowed to get dressed, we were painted with a wide yellow stripe from our skulls right down our spines. It was cold, and we shivered, but we felt clean. My feet were frozen and they wobbled in the wooden clogs that were much too large for me. Blisters and open sores continued to bother me during this time. I was so skinny that I kept wondering, 'How long have I got? Would this ever end?'

All the prisoners were given one thin, flimsy grey blanket each. These were woven from artificial fibre and while they did not give us much warmth, at least they covered our miserable, skeletal bodies. We wrapped them around us. Some of the women created nice styles with their blankets – kimono sleeves, pleats, and, by pulling strands from the edge, they made belts to hold the creations together. Now, we were ready to start marching again and to start the next chapter in our miserable, restricted lives.

We were not told of our next destination. For many months now we had no news of the war. We had no contact with the outside world. No one among the Germans had given us the slightest hint of news and of course they offered no word of encouragement or hope. We kept alive a spark of hope among ourselves and often we used the phrase, 'When the war ends, we will do this or that.' Little did we know that many of us would not live to see the end of the war. But we did not give up.

As we marched out of Trachenberg, it began to snow. The rooftops were white and the tree branches dusted with fine snow, making the scene around us a pretty picture. However, the streets were icy, slushy and slippery. We had to shuffle our way through the slush for more than ten kilometres. By the time we arrived at our destination we were exhausted. We had arrived at a village called Kurzbach. It looked deserted. There were a few small, low-built houses with straw-covered roofs. Near the highway was one larger and nicer-looking cottage and directly across the road was a huge, newly built straw barn. Built of straw panels, it was long and tall with a rounded-off top which made it appear to be a gigantic hangar or beehive. This was to be our housing for the next period of our tormented lives. We were herded inside and there found the walls lined with the familiar three tiered bunks – rows and rows of them waiting for us. It was difficult to climb up to the top bunk, as there were no ladders. The youngest among the prisoners always found it easier to do this so I climbed up and made sure that mother got the one below me.

Each one of us was given a 'sleeping bag'. This brown paper bag was our protection against the cold apart from the thin, frayed grey 'blankets' on each bunk. Normally, paper acts as an insulator and we actually welcomed the bags. However, our bunks were so narrow and constricting that it was almost impossible to get into the bag without tearing it. Within a short time my bag was in tatters, like everyone else's. We made use of the paper by wrapping it around our bodies and stuffing little bits into our clogs.

The top bunk was a good place in winter since it was warmer than the lower bunks, but for me it also meant that I could protect my mother from another torment.

During the night it was sometimes difficult to get out of the bunks to run to the latrine. In our weakened conditions, some of us were simply too weak to get out in time and the person below would often get drenched as the urine dripped freely from the upper bunk. I was lucky that I did not need to use the latrine at night, and so my mother was kept dry and relatively protected. Using the latrine was horrible enough at any time. It was outside the barn and consisted of a very large and deep elongated trench. On each side were two rods and linking these was another rod, no wider than a thin branch on which we sat guarded the whole time by an SS guard. There was no covering or shelter; the latrine was exposed for all to see. As it was freezing cold, our naked and now bony bottoms often froze to the rod adding to our pain. Some women were so terribly weak that they could not get up and would fall into the latrine, drowning in the excrement. It was a horrible and pitiful way to die.

Next to the barn and close to the latrine was a smaller, circular straw building that was called 'the washroom'. The name was another 'joke' since there was no water or basins or anything that could be used to wash. It must have been a requirement for a camp. The Germans were strict about following regulations. There must have been a regulation that stated each camp had to have a washroom though it didn't seem to matter if the washroom was useful or not.

Across from our barn stood a lovely cottage that was the home of the highly decorated SS *Obersturmführer* and his family. Too old for active duty at the front, he was

Hugo Rosenberger, 1918

The wedding of Nelly and Josef Holzer at the Luxor Hotel in Bratislava, 1932. Circled, from left to right: Erwin Weiss, Dr Jakob Weiss, Fritz Weiss, Hugo Rosenberger, Grandfather Ignaczy Weiss, Susi Bardos, Erika Friedlieb, Piroska Rosenberger, Aranka Weiss, Grandmother Helena Weiss.

The wedding of Serena Weiss (sister of Piroska) to Lipot Haas
Circled, from left to right: Hugo Rosenberger, Piroska Weiss, Helena Weiss, Ignaczy Weiss

Hugo Rosenberger, born 13 April 1894 in Bratislava, Czechoslovakia. This photograph was taken in 1924.

Piroska Rosenberger (nee Weiss), born 12 February 1905 in Sala nad Váhom, Czechoslovakia. This photograph was taken in 1924.

Part of the dining room in the Rosenberger house

The Rosenberger's family home at Miczkiewičová Ulica 16 and Špitalská Ulica 45, Bratislava

Piroska Rosenberger with Judith and Olga   *Nanny Annie with Judith and Olga*

At our grandparents house during the holidays, 1933
From left to right: Olga, Miriam, Judith

Judith Rosenberger, deported to Auschwitz-Birkenau, 1942

MINISTRY OF THE INTERIOR

Bratislava, 5th day of March, 1942   Number 14-4-565/1-1942

Re: The Transport of Jews Drafted for Labor

To: The Ministry of Transportation and Public Works
     Railroad Department, B r a t i s l a v a

I request the guarantee and execution of the transport of Jews drafted for
labor, according to paragraph 22 of Law number 198/1941 of the Slovakian Law
of concentrations of labor according to the following conditions:

1) The transported people are treated as groups to which the obligation of
   labor is applied according to the order of the Government with the force
   of Law number 129/1940 of the Slavic Law and hence, they are entitled to
   stop (during the trip) according to the order of the Ministry of Transportation and Public Works, Railroad Department, of 24/4/1941, Number
   1907/3-1941.

2) These transports of labor groups will be sent in full trains, 6 units in
   number. The arrangement of the cars in these trains will be: a service
   car carrying equipment for the physician and the sanitary services, 10
   freight cars for the Jews, 2 freight cars for cargo, one freight car for
   equipment for the transport, one passenger car for the escort, 15 freight
   cars for Jews.

3) The freight cars will be prepared by the railroad management so that they
   will be fit in time of emergency to hold 40 people in each car. This
   preparation of the railroad cars will be carried out by the railroad
   management at the expense of the Ministry of the Interior. One side of
   the freight cars in which the Jews are transported must be tightly and
   securely closed in such a way that it will be impossible to open either
   from inside or outside.

4) The conductor of the train (a railroad clerk of Slovakia) must receive at
   the last station of the transport from the Jewish doctor in the service
   car of the sanitary section a first aid box that is there with the equipment that goes with it (2 stretchers) and, on return, he will deliver them
   at the last station of the train unit (the new loading station of the
   Jewish transport) to the station clerk.

5) The freight cars designated for the transport of Jews must be indicated in
   the train unit according to numbers 1 to 25 (with chalk on the cars). Every
   freight car designated for the transport of Jews will be equipped with one
   covered pail. These pails belong to the supply of the unit. The pails
   must be purchased at the expense of the Ministry of the Interior.

6) It must be ensured that the doors of the freight cars, through which one
   enters the cars, will be able to be opened from inside only to a width of
   10 centimeters and that an additional opening of the doors from within will
   be impossible. These door-openings from outside will be able to be done
   only by the escort services.

An extract from the Slovak Law dealing with the transport of Jews

Female barracks at Auschwitz (AUSTRAL International)

An inmate of Bergen-Belsen at the time of Liberation
(AUSTRAL International)

John Horak, Bratislava, 1947

The wedding of Olga and John Horak on 9 February 1947, under the 'chuppah'

*Olga with her first daughter Evelyn (aged two months)
at Bondi Beach, Sydney, 1950*

Olga in the Hibodress factory, designing blouses, Sydney, 1954

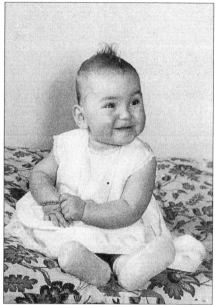

Bozena Bendova with daughter Bohounka

Evelyn Horak, aged 12 months,
4 September, 1951

Hibodress Blouses factory, 1956

From left to right: Olga, Susie (aged 12 months), Evelyn (aged eight), John. Photograph taken on 22 June 1958, Sydney.

Olga Horak in the showroom of Hibodress Blouses, Sydney, 1959

Jonathan's Bar Mitzvah, 1999. From left to right: Anthony Levin, Evelyn Levin (neé Horak), Kirsty Levin, Jonathan Sankey, Susie Berk (neé Horak), Olga Horak, John Horak, Victor Berk.

ideal for home defence. Tall with white hair, this well-groomed SS officer was our Kommandant. Like all the SS, he took his duty of eradicating the enemies of the Reich seriously. And we, a pathetic group of half-starved Jewish women, were the enemies he had to guard. We saw him every morning at roll call where, after receiving the reports from the SS guards, he would address us. '*Ihr Gottverlassenses Volk*' – (You Godforsaken People) – was his favourite opening line. He let us know that, as far as he was concerned, we were not worth spitting on. After months of abuse and torture, it was still de-moralising to be constantly belittled, for it was a constant reminder to us that we were totally at his mercy. We were utterly abandoned.

Two SS women were placed in charge of us and proved to be as cruel and vicious as their male counterparts. They were dressed in the uniform of the female SS, a field grey outfit with a heavy warm cape and the ever-present cane for striking prisoners. Erika, an SS guard, was a very attractive woman with jet-black hair and cold piercing blue eyes and no heart. Else was blond and plain with bandy legs. They were both heartless and brutal. Their uniforms gave them the courage and power to beat and persecute us at their pleasure. The SS appointed a *Stubeneälteste* soon after we arrived in Kurzbach. Frau Auerbach was a cranky, authoritarian woman who reminded me of an unloved schoolteacher. It was her role to continue the harsh treatment of Erika and Else when they had finished their job for the day.

Our daily routine followed the same pattern that I had witnessed in Auschwitz. Roll call at morning and evening formed the two turning points of the day. Standing in our clogs, we sank into the mud and snow during the roll calls. Cold and freezing, we stood waiting to be counted and ordered into our working groups for the day's tasks, and at the end of the day, we were ordered back to our draughty barn at night. Each of us was divided into a numbered work party of 100 women. My mother and I, along with Aunt Franziska and Ruth, belonged to the fourth Hundertschaft. An armed SS man guarded each work party. One of our duties was the early morning distribution of the coffee immediately before roll call. We had to rise early and get the big drum of liquid that was the only sustenance we would have before the evening soup ration, over twelve hours later. Then we were marched off to work about ten kilometres away in a dense pine forest. Accompanying us were the armed SS with their dogs. Well-groomed German Shepherds and jet-black vicious looking Dobermans with big perfect white teeth were trained to watch us. At an order, they could be released to leap and rip us to pieces.

Snow was everywhere and we trudged through it along the road to reach our work site. Over the weeks, perhaps it was months, I cannot remember exactly, we were made to do forced labour in the bitter, freezing cold of the worst winter I have experienced. Given spades and shovels, we were ordered to dig deep trenches. Of course we were never told the purpose of our work, and we never stopped to ask or think about it; that would have attracted another beating. The ground was frozen solid and it was difficult and hard work for feeble, undernourished women. I remember we used wet grass to stuff in our clogs in order to warm and protect our blistered feet. Our exposed hands had no protection and were badly blistered and scratched. Once I fell and injured my knee. The open wound bled profusely which was dangerous. If the guard saw a prisoner on the ground and they were not working, they were clearly malingering and needed a good thrashing. Luckily for me, a fellow inmate bandaged the wound using some dirty rags and pinned them together with a rusty hair-clip. I was in pain and my knee was sprained, but I could walk and at least appear to work.

Once we had finished digging, we had to level out the earth and sand making it into a perfectly level platform. Next, we were ordered to pick up heavy logs from the forest and carry them to the trenches. There, the logs had to be placed carefully next to each other to form some kind of fence. I tried to help my mother by always carrying the heavier and wider end of the log and let her take the tapered, slimmer top end. We always had to work at a fast pace. If we slowed down, or worse, stopped altogether through weakness and sickness, we knew the SS would not hesitate to shoot us. It meant nothing to them. We were an inconvenience that stopped them from getting out of the fierce cold and this antagonised them all the more.

Often, when we had marched back to the camp, exhausted and famished, one of our guards felt it was time to have some fun. He was an evil man, more evil than the others who made my life a misery. He would force us into an open field for 'exercises'. What this meant was we were forced at gunpoint to do push-ups in the snow and slush. Ten or twenty times, up and down followed and then another set as a 'bonus'. He would watch us with a sick grin on his face, enjoying the torture, and if we were not fast enough or displeased him in any way he would kick us down with his hob-nailed boots, pushing us into the slush and mud. The effect of this 'exercise' on already exhausted women, most of whom were like me covered in open sores and chilblains, was awful. When he had enough, he screamed abuse at us and ordered us back into camp.

Not all of us slaved in the forest. A number of prisoners were kept for special tasks around the camp. Organising one of these jobs was highly sought after since it meant being spared from the hell of forced labour in the cold. Serena Kohn was in charge of the *Brotkammer* (bread store) and was responsible for the slicing of the bread ration. Everyday, she would go to the store and slice bread. In the evening, when we returned from the forest, Serena would smuggle extra portions of bread in the rags wrapped around her. It is difficult to imagine the risk she took. If she had been caught, the Germans would have most likely humiliated her with their special treatments.

Hunger drove people to take risks. One woman managed to 'organise' some more bread for herself but was caught by the guard. She was taken away and her head was shaved except for a strip down the middle, making her look like a Mohawk. This was especially degrading since our hair was starting to grow back and the guards must have realised what it meant to us. We had begun to feel human as our scalps sprouted small tufts of hair. Any sign of humanity was to be blotted out by our guards. Another 'lucky' inmate was Lilly Kohn, Serena's daughter. Lilly, who was about a year younger than me, had attracted the attention of the Kommandant. Even though she was half starved like the rest of us, she was very pretty with beautiful dark eyes and short curly hair that was beginning to grow back. The Kommandant ordered her to appear at his house and then made her a maid for his children. This meant that Lilly was indoors for most of the day and since she was with the Kommandant's children, she probably got the opportunity to grab the children's scraps. Both Lilly and her mother survived the Holocaust and we have remained friends ever since.

My cousins Trude and Lilly were with us in the same barn but belonged to a different *Hundertschaft* working somewhere else. At night after roll call and the meagre ration of watery soup and the thin slice of bread given us, we huddled close together in the barn on the muddy floor. We would supplement our starvation diet with a few mushrooms we had found in the forest. Fortunately for us they were not poisonous, and we would carefully divide them among ourselves. There was no lighting, only the moonlight, but that was sufficient for our very modest needs. We sat in circles and talked. Our conversations were simple. We talked about food, exchanging mouth-watering recipes and enjoying verbal cooking sessions. I don't know why but I constantly craved poppyseed covered dumplings. As a child, I had never liked poppyseed, but then, in Kurzbach, I missed what I could not have.

We also composed songs and although we had no paper or pencils we managed to remember the lyrics and tunes. A Polish woman with us used to sing melancholic Yiddish songs in her rich and deep voice. Sometimes we even saw the German guards peeping through the walls and listening to her sing. We had our own *Kurzbach Lied* (Kurzbach Song) which we sang every morning on our march to the forest. The SS even marched in step with the song.

When the day awakes and the sun is smiling
To the forests the column is marching.
In our hearts carrying the sorrow
The forest is dark and the sky is red.
In our pouch we only have a tiny little bread
But in our hearts, in our hearts the sorrow.
Oh Kurzbach! I can't ever forget you
Whatever our fate may be.
Whoever leaves you can only measure
How wonderful freedom is.
Oh Kurzbach! I can't ever forget you
Whatever our fate may be.
We say 'Yes' to life which we treasure
Because the day will come
And we will be free.

I found out later that the *Kurzbach Lied* was not original to our camp. It was sung in other camps with different lyrics. Where the melody came from is a mystery.

The winter of 1944–1945 was severe. It was so cold that I ached and hurt all over. In fact, the cold was so terrible that words cannot describe adequately the suffering it caused. I was dirty and wanted to wash myself so I rubbed snow into my raw skinny body. When I tried to remove the rags from my legs, the skin came off as well. I had open chilblains. My gums were terribly sore and my teeth appeared to dangle from the dark and purple swollen flesh inside my mouth.

I was told to go to the 'hospital' or 'First Aid' room for treatment. It was such an exalted word for such a pitiful room. The camp *Lazarett* was a canvas tent with a single shelf. There may have been a few medicines there, but certainly nothing that could help us in our condition. I was given a lapis stick and I massaged my gums with it but it was not all that helpful.

Stomach-gnawing hunger dominated every waking moment of my day. We constantly talked about food, and my mother used to pass on part of her bread ration to me, claiming she was not hungry. To sacrifice even a small part of your ration made you more likely to succumb to any number of diseases and, of course, the ever-present exhaustion. My mother's sacrifice for me was literally a case of her putting my life before her own. Starvation meant that our bodies were slowly wasting away. Our finger and toenails no longer grew, our skin became waxen and our eyes glazed. It was as though we were living like robots. Energy was needed to keep alive, nothing else. Emotions dried up once we were outside of our barracks. You couldn't afford to show the guards anything other than servile submission for we were their slaves. The guards, rugged up against the cold in thick greatcoats, showed us no compassion or humanity at all. Beatings, whippings, punishment exercises were all a part of the day's work for them.

I don't know exactly how I survived Kurzbach. Everyday I hoped that help would come either from heaven or from the Allies. We prayed that the American and British planes that sometimes flew overhead would drop their bombs on us and so end our misery. But there was no help. The days slipped by, and we became conditioned to the constant violence around us as we performed our tasks like zombies. You learnt not to think because it seemed to make life a little easier.

One day, Christmas decorations appeared on the windows of the Kommandant's house. Now, in between beating and abusing Jewish women, the SS found time to sing Christmas carols rejoicing at the birth of the Jew, Jesus! The world had surely gone mad. It was the Christmas of 1944. One morning after roll call, we were told to form columns, five abreast, and start marching once again towards the unknown.

CHAPTER SEVEN

To Belsen

EVERY MORNING AFTER roll call, we marched towards the forest turning right at the end of the village road. On this morning in early January 1945, however, we were ordered to continue to march straight ahead on the road. They told us we weren't going back to Kurzbach. In the far distance, we could hear the sounds of gunfire and above us we could see planes. The Russians were coming closer and closer. We prayed for bombs to fall on us and end our hellish lives, but they never came.

Visibly weaker and thinner, we were now expected to march in an orderly fashion to our next destination. We were a pathetic group of shaven-headed female prisoners, but we were also 'enemies of the Third Reich'. We were barely able to cover ourselves with strips of old blankets and scraps of brown paper, with numbers painted across our backs. Though we were nearly dead, the SS fussed about ordering us to march like soldiers. Further, they told us that we were to keep marching at all times. 'Anyone who stops or tries to break ranks or sit on the highway will be shot.' And so we marched in this fashion. It was a 'Death March'. Along the icy road we trudged frozen in body with emotionless faces and glazed stares. I don't know if I was afraid any more, I think I had passed caring. If the guard ordered me to march, I marched. If he told me to stop, I stopped. If he shot me, he shot me. At that time, life hung by a thread.

The SS guards were changed frequently at rest stops where they were fed and refreshed. We were given no such rest. Through villages and towns we marched. Sometimes we were taken off the highways and made to walk on rarely used back tracks and dirt roads. We were not alone on the roads. Thousands of German evacuees were also fleeing in the wake of the Russian advance and they clogged the roads with us. I saw innumerable horse-drawn farmcarts, wheelbarrows and old-fashioned carriages laden with luggage, household goods and food. Cans with milk were suspended from the rear of the carts and dangled in front of us. I could see that they had warm, thick blankets and stores of hoarded food. Not one of those thousands ever attempted to throw even a scrap of bread or a potato in our direction. They saw us; they stared at us; they hated us and they knew who we were – Jews. Even with their precious Third Reich crashing down around them, they still hated us.

We marched around the outskirts of the first major German city we came to, Breslau. This meant we had marched for about 125 kilometres. My cousin Lilly had a severe cold with high temperatures and a terrible earache. She was at the end of her strength and together with her sister Trude, she fell out of the column and sat on the edge of the road. We expected the worst. My mother and Aunt Franzi tried to get the two girls up and back into the column, but they would not move. They had taken enough, and were beyond caring what happened to them. The rest of us felt an awful shudder and waited to hear the familiar sound of a machine gun burst. We heard nothing, but kept marching, not knowing if the girls were dead or not. Later, we learnt that the guards were more concerned about getting away from the Russians than killing a couple of Jewish teenage girls. We had no idea the Red Army was so close even though we could hear the sound of the Russian guns shelling German positions. An hour after Lilly and Trude collapsed beside the road, Russian soldiers found them. For them the horror was over and they had survived. It was the first week of January 1945. (Breslau had been declared a 'fortress city' by Hitler, and held out against the Russians until 6 May.)

The rest of us continued to hobble along the roads towards wherever it was the Germans were taking us. I don't know how many days or nights we marched. If I thought about it too much, I would have simply curled up and died. At that point, it would have been so easy. However, I had my mother with me, and I had to live to be with her. We had to survive this ordeal and find the rest of the family. Mother had not given up hope of finding father or Judith. Her strength kept me alive.

Later, we arrived at Gross Rosen about sixty kilometres from Breslau. It was already dark when we reached the huge camp gate. We had come upon a horrible sight. Before us were crowds of people who looked like skeletons, many of them lying on the ground half-naked and practically dead. People were shouting out names: 'Has anyone seen or heard of so and so?' My mother did the same: 'Has anyone seen or heard of my daughter Judith Rosenberger?' There were no replies. It was in Gross Rosen that I renewed contact with one of the most accursed aspects of camp life – lice. When the first lice started to bite into our skin, we brushed them away out of our rags but before long they were back and their numbers only increased. They were everywhere – on our heads, under our arms, crawling all over our bodies. It is a misery that is difficult to describe. Each louse bites into the skin and sucks blood. As they do this, you run the risk of contracting typhus, which in our miserable state was a potentially mortal illness. Our bodies were so weak that even a head cold could be fatal. But the most horrible part was the itching and scratching the lice caused. My skin was raw. One benefit from all of this was the discovery that lice kept the SS at a distance from us. Here was one thing the *Herrenvolk* feared more than us!

We stayed in Gross Rosen for three days. The camp was so overcrowded it was decided it was better for us to keep moving. We were not processed; perhaps they didn't have time. This was the first time we noticed the familiar routines of the camp beginning to break down. The Germans were very particular about observing all the procedures. Everything had to be *Korrekt*. Now the whole system seemed to be disintegrating. After the third day, we were ordered to march out of the camp and take the open road again. Towards evening we arrived in a village square. It was getting dark. At a sandstone fountain, our first ration in days was distributed. The watery soup and small slice of black bread were gobbled up in no time at all. Nearby the SS were eating too. From their aluminium dishes, they wolfed down hot pea soup with chunks of fresh white bread. The soup smelt of smoked meat and the smell lingered in my nose and set my mouth watering. It is strange that after all these years I have no memory of how far I marched, or of the towns and villages I passed through, and yet I can recall what the SS ate in the village square that evening.

The march resumed. People collapsed and died from exhaustion, starvation and the bitter cold. Some had simply given up and once they sat down on the roadside, death would be swift – a bullet from an SS gun or the numbing mercy of the snow. I wonder where we found the strength. How was it possible to still have belief in God? However, we still believed that one day it would all be over. It had to end. But, so many of the women I marched with never saw that day.

It turned out that our next destination was Dresden, nearly 190 kilometres from Gross Rosen. We actually arrived in the city itself, not on the outskirts as we had in Breslau. I saw railway tracks and a little further on I saw an old locomotive puffing at the platform. Behind it were many open cattle cars, winding snake-like along the tracks. After walking for nearly 375 kilometres, we realised the death march seemed to be over. We were pushed and shoved like bits of rubbish, as the SS ordered us onto the open tray-like carriages, which were covered in frozen animal manure, ice and snow. Huddled together, we tried to stay as warm as we could as the freezing wind howled about us and the unbearable cold bit into us as viciously as the lice did. There was one SS man per truck to guard us. They didn't need any more, we were not going to escape. It had taken nearly all our remaining energy to climb up onto the tray. One look at us and people knew we were from a *Konzentrationslager* and Jewish women.

It was snowing and everything around us was white. The train pulled out of the station slowly gathering speed, packed with its human cargo. It did not get very far. We pulled into the main city station of Dresden and stopped. Air raid sirens were screaming around us, whistling their loud deafening shriek. People were scrambling for the shelters. Dresden was crammed with refugees from eastern Germany and ethnic Germans from Poland. An air raid over this city would cause enormous damage and claim many lives. Our brave SS guards, jumped down from the wagons without giving us a second thought. They ran towards the shelters and left us to remain in the open. Overhead, we could see the bombers flying so low we could actually see them clearly. And we saw the bombs fall, raining down on this German city, crammed full of terrified Germans.

The air raid I witnessed that day was one of three 'monster' raids over Dresden in January and February 1945. Three air raids caused cyclonic fire storms in the city and claimed at least 60 000 lives. One of the targets was the marshalling yards near where our train was standing. During the raid, we watched as the bombs fell like manna from heaven. We were not scared even as shrapnel flew around us striking many prisoners and killing more than a few. They died knowing that the

Nazis were all but defeated. We watched, tearfully, with the realisation that perhaps we would survive after all. It was a sign of hope.

Suddenly, the bombing raid was all over and it was quiet. Miraculously, our station was relatively undamaged and within a few minutes our guards returned. The train started to move again and the SS started eating again. No food or water was given to us throughout the whole 500 kilometre journey to Bergen-Belsen. From Dresden our train travelled through Weimar, Halle and Hannover. Since we were in open carriages it was easy to read the names on the station buildings.

I knew nothing about Bergen-Belsen. I did know of the beautiful Lüneburger Heide, but had no idea that amid the dense forest was a notorious Konzentrationslager that stretched for many kilometres disposing of thousands of human beings on a daily basis. The train stopped at Bergen-Belsen and we virtually fell out of the carriages. Many among us had died during the journey but because of the intense cold and the cramped conditions, they somehow had remained upright among the living. They were pulled out with us.

By now we were very sick. Whatever body fat I had on me had disappeared many months ago. My bones stuck out, my breasts had all but disappeared, my teeth were loose in my mouth, I was covered with open weeping sores and I crawled with lice. My eyes were sunken in their sockets, the little hair I had was patchy, and I could barely stand upright let alone stand straight. And yet, I was not as sick as the inmates I saw standing before me in Belsen.

Inside the camp were rows and rows of wooden huts standing in what looked like endless lines along the camp roads. I think we were taken to *Lager 8*, the 'Large Women's Camp'. It had been established in the autumn of 1944 as prisoners were evacuated to Belsen from the frontline areas. *Lager 8* was divided into different huts, which were so overcrowded that mother and I could only find a small place on the floor where we barely stretched out, and fell asleep. The camp was the worst I had been in – starved, naked bodies were everywhere. *Lager 8* was worse than Birkenau, and in the months prior to Liberation it got even worse.

The next day we received our 'rations' – black water, a small slice of black bread and, if we were lucky, the watery soup after roll call at night. The roll calls continued. Why did they bother? Did it matter to them if there were fewer of us in the rows to be counted? We were not meant to survive anyway. No one deported was meant to survive! We had seen too much; we knew too much and we were Jews who had no right to live.

That day, my mother and I, along with a few others, were taken from our group and sent to a small room called the *Schälküche* – the peeling kitchen. Planks of rotting timber were placed on tin drums for us to sit on. Large bags of huge, grey, dusty turnips were tipped onto the floor and we had to peel them with blunt knives. The peeled turnips were then dropped into empty drums or buckets and taken away. We were ordered not to eat any of the turnips or the peels. It was another horrible torture to have to peel these vegetables and not be able to hide even a few scraps to eat later on. But I had been in the camps long enough to know what would happen if I was caught and now I was determined to survive. I stayed hungry. I don't know for whom the turnips were peeled and cooked. They weren't fit for human consumption. Then, one day, my hunger won and overcame me. I was in the Schälküche and while sitting on my wooden plank I noticed a turnip peel hanging on a ledge near the floor. I had to have it. I reached over to grab it, but the guard saw me and stabbed me in the upper arm with his bayonet. I didn't scream, I simply held my arm and tried to ignore the horrible pain. I considered myself lucky to have gotten away with a stabbing. What I dreaded was being taken to the Prügelstrafe where the guard could have enjoyed himself flogging me to death. After that incident, I never tried to get a peel again.

My health continued to decline. A typhus epidemic had broken out in January 1945. By the time we arrived, it had spread throughout the camp. My mother and I caught the disease almost immediately. The acute diarrhoea, vomiting and dehydration left us with little strength. We were too weak to move, and this meant that I would be unable to get rations for us. My glands were swollen with what was later diagnosed as diphtheria. Others suffered with tuberculosis and cholera. This epidemic of sickness was 'normal life' in Belsen. Outside the barracks, piles of bodies grew into small mountains waiting to be 'processed'. The sheer number of prisoners had made the camp routines buckle. Bodies were not being burnt or buried. Work details were not formed. It was bedlam. The stench was beyond belief – urine, excrement, vomit and rotting flesh hung in the air all around us. So great was the cold that people had torn up parts of their bunks for firewood so that sometimes the bunk itself collapsed. If someone died during the night, the body remained next to the living until morning before being dragged outside for roll call. Bodies were often stripped of 'valuables' — shoes or boots, bits of string or wire, a spoon or tin bowl — anything that could be salvaged and reused. It was all part of survival. If you didn't try to stay alive, you would die. And since we saw death every waking moment of the day, it was as common as breathing.

In the final weeks before the Liberation, conditions in the camp declined further. The bread ration was reduced to less than a slice a day and then stopped completely. Our only food was a cup of soup and then the water stopped. There was no drinking water for the 60 000 prisoners in Belsen for nearly a week. I believe that the Germans deliberately cut the water supply. They were determined to kill as many of us as possible through 'natural' means so that they would not be accused of murder! Our morale was completely broken. At this time, I believed we were all dying. We had no news of the war and no idea where the nearest Allied troops were. There was no fighting around Belsen and we didn't see planes flying overhead.

On 15 April 1945, we lined up for roll call as usual. Mother and I were very weak as we waited, believing that the SS were taunting us with sudden changes to the routine. Suddenly, we were aware of noise all around us. There was shooting and gunfire and the sounds of trucks and tanks. The commotion got louder and louder getting close to the camp. No SS guards appeared. Something drastic was happening. It was exciting but nerve-racking at the same time. Was it all a trick? Did the Germans plan to kill us all at the last minute. Is that why we could hear tanks?

We saw the tanks! They were not the grey German Panzers but green British vehicles (we did not know this at the time). All we knew was that the tanks were not German, so they must be from the Allies. We were liberated! We had survived! We had beaten Hitler! We were alive! These feelings filled my heart but I was so weak I could not even cheer. Around me, I could hear sounds of hysterical laughter and weeping penetrating and echoing in the grey, cold, misty polluted air. The feeling of liberation was subdued in Belsen. We were too weak to celebrate and besides the SS guards were still armed and prowling about along with the Hungarian SS and they were still killing prisoners even after the British entered the camp.

The British were interviewing the Kommandant, SS Hauptsturmführer Josef Kramer. Originally, Kramer's plan was to seek a 24-hour truce with the British claiming a typhus epidemic as the excuse to keep the Allies out of Belsen. What Kramer wanted was time to destroy documents and most likely kill 'prominents' – special prisoners who had been kept in isolation for political reasons. Fortunately, the British refused the request. They had seen enough of Belsen to sum up what kind of men they were dealing with. When they entered the camp, British soldiers saw the sickening confusion. There were thousands of near-naked starved skeletons moving about the mountains of decomposing bodies stacked like corkwood. It was too much for many of these battle-hardened men.

The British acted swiftly. Hours after entering the camp, they brought DDT in by the truck load and we were lined up to be dusted and deloused. They attached wide hoses to the truck engines and we were decontaminated and deloused with the white powder that settled on us like snow. Although we looked even more horrible than before, the maddening itching stopped almost immediately as the lice died. The relief was wonderful. The British restored the water supply which allowed us not only drinking water but also the opportunity to wash ourselves for the first time in months. After so many years of degradation, we were now able to feel the some sense of human dignity returning to our lives.

The British left food outside the barracks. Those who were too weak and too ill to move went without. They died of starvation. There was no one to feed them. Those of us who were able to get to the food were so weak that it was all we could do to feed ourselves. We simply had no reserve energy. Throughout the barracks, we heard the heartrending cries of *Essen, essen!* (Food, food!). Disaster had struck again. Our bodies had grown accustomed to starvation diets and unhealthy food. We were physically unable to eat even the most basic foodstuffs without a long recuperation. There was no fresh food so we were given army rations. These canned foods were too rich for our feeble digestive systems. Powdered milk was distributed but caused outbreaks of vomiting and diarrhoea. Later, biscuits and baked beans were handed out, but I couldn't eat them as my mouth was full of terrible ulcers and I couldn't swallow without great difficulty. It would take months of healing before I would be able to eat anything that approached a 'normal' meal.

However, I was now a 'survivor'. I was no longer a prisoner, but not yet free. There was much that had to be done before we could consider the journey home. For a start, we were so weak that we were not yet able to live without immediate medical attention. The British wanted to register us all on the first day of Liberation. A makeshift tent was set up in the grounds of the camp. At the table was an officer with two or three uniformed officers behind him. I went with my mother to the tent 'office' and we stood patiently in a line waiting for our turn. We arrived at the tent and walked in facing the officer behind the table. My mother went first. She gave her full name and other details and told the officer that she wanted to be repatriated home to Bratislava. I followed and did the same. Each of us were then issued with a small white Displaced Persons card which we had to sign. My mother was so weak she could not hold the card firmly in her hands. I had to hold the card for her. We then made our way out of the tent. Then what I dreaded most happened. My mother collapsed. I tried to get her up but nurses came and gently pushed me aside. They brought a stretcher and lifted mother onto it. She lay there ashen coloured and made no response to me. I placed my hands over her short dark stubs of hair and tried to speak to her, softly, but she did not respond.

I begged her to say something to me, and kept saying over and over: 'Mama, please do not leave me now. We are free. We are going home. Please do not leave me alone!' It was in vain. My mother had survived Auschwitz, a death march from Kurzbach to Dresden, the journey to Belsen and four months in that cesspool, only to die moments after being registered as a survivor.

I was completely alone. I had lost my mother forever.

CHAPTER EIGHT

The Journey Home

I HAD LOST HER. My mother was only forty years old, and I was eighteen. We had survived the entire war together and now she was taken from me on the day of Liberation when we were looking forward to going home. I followed the nurses who had placed my mother on a stretcher but they stopped me and said I could not go with them. I remember that I stood there outside the tent for a long time clutching the two Displaced Persons cards watching as my mother was carried away. Piroska Rosenberger became another victim of the Holocaust. She was just another body with no name to be buried in a mass grave covered in lime and sand. I returned to my barrack in a daze.

The next day I went to search for my mother's body. My cousin Ruth joined me. We went to the place where she had been taken, but no one could tell us where she was. No one knew. She had no name or marker, nothing to distinguish her from the thousands of bodies lying in makeshift heaps around the camp. I kept trying, but it was in vain. I felt an enormous wave of guilt that I lived while my mother lay somewhere unknown amidst this hellhole. I made a great mistake by leaving her to be taken away, even though I knew she was dead. To this day, I have never come to terms with the loss of my mother. I carry this pain with me always.

Added to the emotional pain was the pain of my own physical condition. I was still sick from fever caused by typhus and diphtheria. But I kept looking for my mother's body. As we passed through the camp streets, I recognised an old friend from Budapest, Fritzi Fried, who hid with her parents in Kresz Geza Utca before they were captured and deported. She was looking for survivors from her family too. It was difficult to recognise people since we all looked so appalling. Some, however, had survived better than others. I even encountered Eta H, the Kapo from Auschwitz. She had most likely been evacuated to Bergen-Belsen during the last days of Auschwitz. Eta looked well and was among the first group of DPs to be repatriated.

As I stumbled about the camp streets, I saw another huge pile of bodies, naked and decomposing, awaiting burial. Many of the corpses had been there for weeks and the stench was terrible. Fortunately, the cold weather helped slow the rotting, but it was still a hideous sight and smell. Sights such as this were so much a part of my day-to-day existence that it meant little to me. But, the memory of those days is impossible to forget.

On another mountain of human bodies I found a treasure. A woollen camel-coloured overcoat was lying on the ground waiting, so it seemed, for me. I hesitated at first, then picked it up and slipped it on and it fit me well. I wrapped it around me and secured it with a matching belt. I kept on walking and reached the camp gate, and for the first time since I arrived in Belsen four months before, I walked out of the camp.

The barbed wire had been torn down in many places, but I wanted to walk through the gate as a free woman. Once outside the confines of the camp area, I could not believe what I saw. Nestled among the trees and surrounded by well-tended gardens were rows of private houses standing in very civilised streets. These houses were now occupied by Allied troops. Sentries guarded the entrances to the houses, but that did not stop me. I walked up to the front door of one of the villas and knocked. A group of French Canadian officers invited Ruth and I to come in. My French came in handy and I was able to converse with them comfortably. In the centre of the large room was a table and chairs and in the centre of the table was a basket with the most beautiful red apples. I looked at them, and I knew exactly what I wanted. I made up my mind and did not hesitate to ask the officer if we could have some apples. He was willing to give Ruth and myself one each in return for a small favour. Most of the houses were decorated with British Union Jacks, but the French Canadians wanted to show off the French Tricolour. Unfortunately, they did not have a flag. So the officer asked me to make one for them. He provided fabrics and the threads and a needle and I sat down and started to sew. It took a long time to finish what turned out to be a large French flag since I wanted to do the best job I could. I wanted the hand stitching to be neat and also strong. I used small backstitching on the seams to make sure it would not fray. The officer seemed satisfied and Ruth and I walked out with our well-earned red apples.

It was already getting dark when we returned to our barrack in the camp. I wanted to eat my apple but I could not manage to bite or swallow. My gums were sore and my throat hurt. Survivors who were reasonably fit, were preparing for repatriation and the journey home to liberated villages and towns where they hoped others from their families would be waiting. Aunt Franzi and Ruth, who had been registered on the same day as my mother and I, were ready for their trip. They had learnt through the Red Cross that Uncle David and Marc had survived and were already at home in Bratislava. They were one of the few very lucky families to have survived the Holocaust intact. Aunt Franzi showed no concern for me at all. Only Ruth came to me and said goodbye. But as she drew closer to me, to my surprise, she stripped me of my coat, put it on and then left. Evidently she thought I was going to die and so I would have no need for such a good warm coat. I was too sick to resist or struggle. I fell back to the floor and huddled in my rags.

I would have lain there and given up except for what happened next. Eta H, the former Kapo, saw me and covered me with a blanket. The blanket had been hers in Auschwitz and she no longer needed it as she was returning to her former home. Eta's 'particular rug' was a grayish-black and dirty-white striped blanket, coarsely woven. On a closer examination, I saw it was made of human hair and recycled old fibre. I considered the blanket to be very precious and it was now the only thing to keep me warm. With my precious blanket, I somehow clambered up onto an upper bunk. I had a high temperature and suffered from dysentery. I had no strength to leave the bunk. I could not climb down let alone get back up again. I lay in my own waste and lost consciousness. I called for my mother, crying from the overwhelming sense of loss, loneliness and misery.

I would have stayed there and most likely died had it not been for a number of former prisoners, doctors and nurses who now worked as medical staff. I was taken from my bunk and brought to the camp sickbay which was a white-washed two-storey house within the camp. Every room was filled with very sick people. There were no beds, so we lay on the floor on stretchers that had been elevated off the floor. The stretchers were clean and we had clean sheets. I had my blanket but I could not use it, so it lay folded alongside my clogs next to my stretcher. The medical staff did what they could to make our suffering bearable but there was no medication and the task was enormous.

When the nursing staff weighed me, I was only twenty-nine kilos. They decided that I was too ill for the stretched resources of the camp sickbay. I had to be transferred to the nearest town hospital. This was arranged and I was soon picked up and taken by an army ambulance to Celle, which was the nearest city to Bergen-Belsen. There I was deposited in the city's State Hospital. I found myself in a very large ward, with perhaps thirty beds, all occupied with sick Germans. I had terrible abdominal pains and was calling for help or attention, but the German nurses ignored me. They did not come to clean me, nor did they come to feed me. They may have feared contracting typhus or diphtheria, but I believe the real reason was that I was a Jewess. I came from Bergen-Belsen some time in the last days of April 1945, the war had not yet ended, and there were many Germans who still saw Jews as not worthy of life. I was a sick Jewess in a German hospital bed expecting treatment. There was no compassion though they gave me a thimble full of opium to keep me quiet.

I slept for most of the time or drifted in and out of consciousness. I was woken up one day and saw a military priest next to my bed. He was visiting the sick. The Padre wore his British uniform with the crucifix on his lapel and a prayer book in his hands. He spoke to me in English and luckily I understood all he said. He was friendly and told me that he was there to give me the last rites! I was surprised. Despite being so ill, I understood what he was saying and I responded immediately. Politely but firmly I told him I was Jewish and that I had been brought to the hospital from Bergen-Belsen concentration camp.

I did not need Christian 'last rites' since I was Jewish, and 'Anyhow,' I said, 'I am not going to die!'

The Padre was a good man and he said to me, 'Of course, just tell me what can I do for you.' We started to talk and I asked him whether they had a field Rabbi. 'Yes. We have a Rabbi in our unit.'

'Well,' I pleaded, 'Can you please arrange with the Rabbi to get me out of here and have me returned to the sickbay in Bergen-Belsen because the German nurses do not look after me. I do not want to stay here in this hospital!'

Within a short time an army ambulance arrived with a Rabbi who also wore his uniform, and the Padre. I was driven back to the camp's sickbay. I asked the Rabbi to notify my Aunt Irene in Tel Aviv to let her know I was alive. Somehow I remembered her address, 20 Spinoza Street, Tel Aviv. The Rabbi sent a message for me. Back in the sickbay, I was sharing a room with many other sick patients. Most of them were sick with tuberculosis. They coughed all the time and many died during the days I was there. All the suffering overwhelmed me. We were liberated, supposedly free people, and yet the suffering went on. Would it ever end? Would there be anyone in Bratislava if I ever got back there?

A former inmate, Dr Winterberger, was in charge of the sickbay. He was a kind man, formerly from Prague, and he had elected to stay in Bergen-Belsen for a while to try to help the sick. Since there was no medicine available, he suggested I be given injections of glucose. The needles penetrated my skinny body and I screamed with pain. Many British and Canadian soldiers from the Liberation units came to visit the sick survivors. I was used as a 'special showpiece'. The nurses (or rather, orderlies) often lifted the sheets to show my shriveled skeletal body, which was covered with boils and hives. One Canadian sergeant, Harry Altro, visited me regularly. He came almost daily and brought me things I hadn't seen in many months. Talcum powder and soap were like gifts from heaven to me, and I welcomed them gratefully. However, I was far too ill to eat the food Harry brought. Harry lives today in Montreal and I was lucky to establish contact with him years later.

I was alone again. Aunt Franzi and my cousin left while I was still deathly ill. A Red Cross parcel arrived for Aunt Franzi from her brother in London. It was passed on to me, and I kept it, unopened, until I arrived in Bratislava many months later. During the following weeks, I was lethargic and depressed. I had no plans and my fate lay in the hands of others. I was too weak to get off my stretcher and I could not stand or walk on my own. There appeared to be no future for me but somehow, I knew I had to live.

The weather grew warmer but our windows were kept closed because of the foul smell from the mountains of decomposing bodies that still lay about the camp. The Allied soldiers forced the former SS men and women to clean up the camp. They were made to bury the dead in mass graves. Thousands of skeletal bodies were lain underground and covered with lime and sand. The British made sure the local German civilians witnessed the product of 'Nazi Kultur'. Most said nothing as they watched the piles of human corpses being loaded into trucks by their former SS comrades.

The war ended officially on 8/9 May 1945. I had been a free human being for nearly a month. By July, many of the survivors were already on their way home. Bergen-Belsen was to be evacuated and destroyed. The Union Jack never flew over the camp. A British Colonel explained that the British flag does not stand for cruelty and bestiality; that was for the banner of the Nazis. All the patients in the sickbay were to be moved along with everyone else still in the camp. Belsen was to be set on fire and razed to the ground. One morning, after being sponged down, I was given a clean hospital gown. I was to take my blanket and clogs and with the other patients on stretchers was taken by ambulance to the railway station. There we were lifted aboard a military hospital train that was to take us to the State Hospital in Pilzen. Former SS men, now prisoners of war and still wearing their field grey uniforms, now wore white armbands marked with a red cross. Some of them wore white sanitary coats. These same men who behaved like wild beasts only a short time ago, who delighted in inflicting torture and misery upon me were now to collect us from the sickbay and carry us to the ambulances. At the station, our former tormentors had to help us aboard the train. I was too weak to resist or say anything. When they spoke to me in polite and warm terms, I could not speak in return. Oh, how the world had changed and oh, how their 'compassion' stank of insincerity!

We did not leave them behind once the train left Belsen. The ex-SS men travelled with us. The British had forced them to act as our attendants for the journey to Pilzen. They distributed the food prepared for us and were responsible for keeping us clean and comfortable. Most of us found our digestive systems still unable to cope with anything other than the most basic foods. We had no strength to climb down from the bunk and make our way to the toilet. Consequently, we were constantly, soiling ourselves and our bed linen. It was the duty of the Germans to change the linen and ensure we were comfortable. This they did without complaint. They had been told that we were to be delivered to the hospital in Pilzen clean and safe. When we arrived, the city was still occupied by the American Liberation forces. It was my first visit to the city so well known for its famous beer. Army ambulances were waiting for us at the railway station. One by one, the sick survivors were lifted from the bunks in the carriages and lowered from the train onto stretchers. I screamed with pain as the German orderly touched me while he carried me. Only the hospital gown covered my nudity. My clogs and blanket were my only possessions, and Aunt Franzi's Red Cross parcel.

The State Hospital of Pilzen was a very busy institution at that time. It was overcrowded and it soon became clear that they were not expecting patients in such poor health as we were. Nonetheless, we were admitted. The nursing sisters in most Czechoslovakian public hospitals at that time were Roman Catholic nuns. They were highly dedicated women and the best nurses who went about their duties with great compassion and kindness. When we arrived, they were somewhat stunned because none of them had ever expected that the patients from Germany would look so terrible.

Most of us from that transport were admitted to the ward for contagious diseases. I was brought to a ward for tuberculosis patients.

A slightly built, elderly nun with a kind, smiling face took me in a wheelchair and put me in a small private room. She stopped and showed me a single bed and said, 'My dear child, you are so lucky, you can occupy this bed now. It became available a short while ago; someone just passed away.' I should have been happy to be in a private room with a bed and a pillow and blankets but I was not.

The fact that the previous patient had just died of tuberculosis left me feeling very sad. The sheets had not been changed and that made me hesitant. Somehow, I had the feeling that I was not sick with tuberculosis. I didn't have the symptoms of sweating and coughing like the others did whom I saw suffering and dying. I decided not to obey and did not take the empty bed, which stood there so inviting and waiting for me. At the same time, I thought, 'What right did I have to reject a bed?' After all, I had not slept in a bed for a long time. Did it matter whether the sheets were changed or not? Instead, I nestled into a wicker armchair which stood in the corner. It was not very comfortable. I covered myself with my blanket and with the clogs on my skinny feet, I fell asleep. I stayed in the cane chair for the next three days and nights, sleeping and resting.

Eventually someone collected me and brought me to the X-ray room. Several X-ray pictures later, I was declared to be free from tuberculosis. There was another problem. The doctors and nurses could not decide what to do with me. I had to be removed and placed in a different ward. Professor Resler, the doctor in charge, took one look at me and sent me to the Dermatology ward. I remember feeling an overwhelming sadness. It was as though, as I slowly regained some strength, the reality of my situation kept me weak. The fact that I was completely alone was overwhelming. I had no one to speak to and despite the kind treatment from the nuns, I still felt as though I was an object manipulated by others.

Before I was taken to the Dermatology ward, the nurses took me to a bathroom. Naked, I stood in the tub and waited. My knees buckled, and I had to be supported to stay upright. The nurses brought a pink lotion, emptied it into a basin and painted me with it using a mop – top to toe. I looked in the mirror and what I saw was funny, but I couldn't laugh. I could hardly believe it was me. I was a pink skeleton, with bulging starry eyes, teeth hanging from my mouth, with short stubs of hair on my skull. I had no eyebrows or eyelashes. When I touched the tufts of hair on my head, it stayed on my hands, falling out because of the typhus.

I was given a clean hospital gown and wheeled into a large ward where I was placed into a clean bed. I had no idea of the types of illnesses treated in the Dermatology ward. I quickly found out that most of the female patients were infected with sexually transmitted diseases. They were rape victims. Many different armies passed through Pilzen during and after the war. During the German occupation, the Nazis wined and dined the women, and the women succumbed. The Russians came with no subtleties. They just said 'Davaj' and the women had no choice. The Americans came and brought luxuries – chewing gum, chocolates and nylon stockings. The women were lured, though most probably went voluntarily and ended up with these diseases.

Only one other woman in the ward was, like me, suffering from something other than a sexually transmitted disease. Bozena Bendová occupied the bed next to me. She was a hairdresser and her hands had developed a form of eczema from the chemicals she worked with. Bozena was horrified when she looked at me. I was the first Jewish person this practicing Catholic woman had ever met. 'Are we not all the same human beings, regardless of our religion?' she wondered. I had met my first true friend since the horrors began. Bozena had daily visitors and she enjoyed their company and appreciated the extra home-cooked food they brought along. The hospital food was plain, boring and limited. This realisation was a sure sign that I was starting to recover my health. I had not seen home-cooked food for so long and Bozena noticed how I stared at the food that her mother brought in a basket covered with a red and white checked tea towel. The smell was delicious and tickled my nostrils. I saw dumplings, sprinkled with poppy seed and icing sugar. It was exactly as I had dreamed in the concentration camp. Bozena always shared her food with me. The dumplings were the 'jewel in the crown' and I enjoyed them thoroughly. Although my appetite returned slowly and I could not eat anything more than small portions, I was delighted to be able to eat some 'normal' food.

I could not get out of bed and my feet started to swell. They were full of water and infected – oedema, I was told. I thought the skin would burst at any time. The rest of my body was still covered with a red rash, but my temperature was normal and once again I could think clearly. I had long conversations with Bozena, my new friend. This was so important for it helped me to re-establish contact with the world I had left when I was arrested. Two weeks later, Bozena was told that she was cured and would be discharged from the hospital. On her departure day, she dressed, packed her overnight bag and with tears in her eyes, sat on my bed and said goodbye.

Then she left the ward and walked down the corridor.

Only a few minutes later, she returned and walked straight to my bed and said, 'Olga, take your blanket and clogs. I cannot leave you here on your own. I will take you home with me.' This was like a dream to me. I did not know what to do. I hesitated for a while until Professor Resler was called to look at me and was asked for his permission for me to be discharged. He agreed.

Now, weighing thirty-two kilograms and still frail, I stepped into my clogs and wrapped my blanket about me. My water-filled feet filled the oversized clogs that were scratched and worn after having travelled hundreds of kilometres through the harsh winter conditions and over the icy roads. I carefully took my first steps, supported by Bozena and her brother who had come to fetch us. I was going home with friends. Bozena lived in a 'self-contained' apartment on the ground floor of an old building. The room served as her bedroom, lounge room, dining room and kitchen all in one. A double bed stood against the wall. There was a settee, a table and two chairs. In the corner there was a stove and an old-fashioned basin with running cold water. The toilet was outdoors in the courtyard and was used by several other tenants as well. When we arrived at her apartment, it looked tidy with the bed prepared and inviting. It had clean linen over feather pillows and a comfortable quilt. I was to share the bed with Bozena who placed me there soon after we arrived at her home. I did not realise how terribly weak I still was. I was covered in sweat and fell asleep immediately.

Bozena returned to her hairdressing work, but prepared everything for me before she left early in the morning. She locked the door behind her while I slept. I stayed in bed for most of the day and only got up to go outside to the toilet. It was difficult. I had to crawl on all fours many times. Bozena always brought some food home which was still scarce and mostly available in exchange for coupons or on the black market. Bozena was determined to nurse me back to full health by feeding me with nourishing things. Dumplings were on the daily menu. She was very competent at making the most perfect Czech dumplings. They were as light as a feather! The recipe Bozena taught me was a well-guarded family secret. 'Never cut them with a knife,' she would say, 'that squashes and flattens them. Use a white cotton thread instead.' Bozena was a good-natured woman. She would try to cheer me up by dancing and teaching me songs. *Koline Kolinecku* and *Biely Sokol Biely Vtak* were two songs she taught me. I also brushed up on my Czech language.

After a short time I was now ready to establish contact with a Jewish Office in order to find out how I could travel back home to Bratislava. Bozena got me the necessary information about the office I would have to contact. There was, however, the problem of getting to the office, and of what to wear. I suddenly realised I had nothing to wear and that I could not go out in my hospital gown. The weather was still mild since it was September 1945. I took the thin grey military blanket which I had on the train from Bergen-Belsen to Pilzen and looked at it for a while. I did not need it any longer and therefore I could cut it up and sew it into a suit. I made up my mind. I placed the blanket on the floor and started cutting out a skirt, on the bias, flared with only two seams, one on either side. Not much was left for a jacket. It would have to be a sleeveless vest. The next few days were spent sewing and stitching up my new suit. It looked all right. I was only concerned about my skinny arms and legs which were not a very pretty sight at all.

After a few days, I was ready to leave the room. Dressed in my new suit, I had more confidence and I did not worry about not having shoes or stockings. My clogs would have to serve me for a few weeks to come. I found myself walking through the streets of Pilzen. I had to be careful to walk close to buildings on the footpath. My feet were still very swollen with oedema and my legs were weak. When my knees buckled I fell to the ground. With great difficulty, I pulled myself up, holding onto anything I could grab to help me. I was concerned about people who saw me. Maybe they thought I was drunk or maybe they thought I was a hobo or not quite 'normal'.

I found the office of the Jewish community centre. It was a small room sparsely furnished with an old table and a chair. It was the Joint or HIAS emergency office. Mrs Tanzer, a Czech Jewess, was in charge and she interviewed me and did not hesitate to offer help. She promised to obtain two train tickets to Bratislava, one for me and one for Bozena. I was overcome with excitement but also with extreme concern. I had no explanation for why I felt homesick. I guess I had a spark of hope and thought that maybe some of my closest beloved ones would have survived and returned? I knew that Aunt Franzi was already at home. However, I had written to the family in Bratislava, advising them that I was on my way home, but had not heard anything from them. That hurt me deeply. I felt betrayed and abandoned. If not for the encouragement of Bozena, I would have lost all faith and trust in humanity. Bozena knew that I had nothing to offer her in return for all her love and care of me, and yet she never stopped giving it to me. She never expected anything in return.

One day, I received a letter from my Aunt Frieda and Uncle Ernie Bardos. They were relatives of mine on my mother's side of the family. They were survivors of Theresianstadt. Aunt Frieda had heard from other family members that I had survived and was recuperating in Pilzen. Since the rest of the family indicated they were unable to collect me or even write to me because of the approaching Jewish High Holy Days, she and Uncle Ernie invited me to join them as soon as possible. It seemed like a miracle. I was now convinced that there was someone above looking after me.

Bozena was ready to accompany me on my trip to Bratislava. We had our tickets and we set a departure date in mid-September 1945. Bozena had taken time off from her work and looked forward to the trip as she had never been to Bratislava before. It was also a part of her commitment to me to take me home safely. I wore my grey suit, the flared skirt and sleeveless vest, and my clogs on my water-filled feet. I had left the rug Eta had given me, in Bozena's apartment. I carried no luggage. Somehow I stopped worrying about my baldness. I knew I looked ugly next to Bozena who was pretty and well-groomed. First, we took the train to Prague where we had to wait until a connecting train took us to Bratislava that night. It was a sunny day and so we waited in a park across from the railway station. We sat on a bench on the green lawn. It was a perfect place for us to rest while we waited for the next train. We sat down, chatted away and watched the people pass by. Prague was teeming with military men, mostly Russian soldiers but also Americans and British. They all enjoyed the beauty of the ancient historical city. They also enjoyed the hospitality of the liberated Czech people who had suffered for many years during the occupation and the war.

A well-dressed Russian officer stopped in front of the bench where we sat and started a conversation with Bozena. She asked him for the correct time. He pushed up the sleeve of his uniform jacket and to my great surprise proudly displayed about ten watches. Bozena was not shy. She boldly told him to give her one of the watches. He couldn't possibly need ten, and she didn't have even one. 'Yes,' he said, 'Charasho – why not. But come with me for a short walk first.' Bozena left the park bench and went for the 'short walk' with the Russian officer. I had no idea where they went, but when she returned an hour later she showed me a beautiful gold bracelet watch which the Russian had given her. No questions were asked. Whatever Bozena did was all right with me.

We finally boarded the train at eight o'clock that evening. Although it was a passenger train, there were no seats in the carriages. Instead there were wooden benches. I was so tired I fell asleep very quickly and did not notice the uncomfortable benches. When I think that I had travelled in open cattle cars, this train was quite a contrast and not all that uncomfortable.

CHAPTER NINE

Return to Bratislava and John

WE ARRIVED IN Bratislava the next morning and, to my great surprise and joy, we were met by my cousin Thomas. He had survived the horror of the camps and, like me, was now an orphan. He was cared for and looked after by the Bardos family. Aunt Frieda and Uncle Ernie Bardos lived on Richardova Ulica in a modern multistoried apartment building. They were on the fourth floor which was a long way up stairs since there was no elevator. They lived in what would be described today as a 'bachelor apartment' with one large bedroom, a small kitchen with a dining niche and a bathroom. Thomas was able to move into his own parental home, which was occupied by strangers but he managed to share a room there, while the Bardos family warm-heartedly supplied him with home-cooked food.

My aunt and uncle were wonderful people. Although they were visibly shocked when they saw me, nonetheless, they treated me as though I were their own child. I was made to feel welcome and wanted. Zsuzsi, their daughter, along with her husband Jeno (Eugene), also looked after me. I slept on a daybed in their bedroom and Bozena slept on a mattress in the niche near the kitchen. Although I was now with family, I was very shy and withdrawn. I didn't speak readily to anyone and tried to stay out of the way. I tried to help with the few household chores I could manage. The years of hiding and being hunted, the torture of the camps and the treatment I received there, had left terrible scars that would take years to heal. I was blessed to have such understanding people as Bozena and my aunt and uncle.

Bozena stayed with us for three days before she had to return to Pilzen. I had grown very fond of her. The weeks we had spent together had forged a special bond between us and I promised I would stay in touch and visit her as soon as possible. How could I ever repay her for her unselfish humanity and her love towards me? To me Bozena was a saint. Saying goodbye was so hard.

Uncle Ernie was a successful businessman who had been able to resume his work after returning from Theresianstadt. He was well off financially and was generous with his money. He was a lovable and gentle man. Aunt Frieda was equally loving and also a great cook! She made wonderful food. After not having eaten properly for so long, I enjoyed everything she made and I grew stronger each day. Now that I was back in Bratislava, I had to try and remember where my parents had left things for safekeeping. I looked up former neighbours and friends and went to see my family house on Spitalska Ulica. I was in for a nasty surprise when I arrived at the house that had been my home for so many years. A few family members had already made their home there though some had moved on to different places. I was hoping to be able to move into one room, but was told in no uncertain terms that the place was too crowded. There was no room for me. I would have to go elsewhere. The hurt I felt at this rebuke is difficult to express. I had survived Auschwitz and Belsen only to be told I could not stay in my own home with my family. So I left.

In the courtyard, I found my much-loved and cherished bicycle. It was neglected but still workable. The tyres were intact and so I hopped on it and rode away returning to the Bardos family in Richardova Ulica. I never pursued the matter of returning to Spitalska Ulica. Another chapter in my life was closed.

War does terrible things to people. My parents had left some valuables in the care of Mr and Mrs Suhajda. When I went to see them and asked for the things my parents had left with them, Mrs Suhajda, who had the honorific title 'Countess', looked me in the eye and said everything was gone having been taken by the Russians. The Countess obviously thought I would leave, but I noticed a porcelain figurine on her mantelpiece. It was the 'Cow and Calf', a piece that my father had bought home from one of his trips to Copenhagen. I told the lady that the figurine was mine, walked calmly to the mantelpiece and took it. Later, I saw Mrs Suhajda walking in the city wearing the fur coat that had belonged to my mother. I said and did nothing. There is only so much betrayal one can absorb.

Good people have to be remembered too. Two elderly ladies who had heard of my survival and return sought me out. They brought with them embroidered napery and bed linen which my mother had asked them to keep for her. These ladies came from aristocratic backgrounds and were members of the German Cultural Circle. They asked me to help them. People of German descent were being forcibly relocated, expelled from Czechoslovakia. They were terrified of being deported to Germany. Hoping for my help, the sisters asked me to write a reference for them stating they had not been Nazis and had assisted victims of the German occupation. I wrote the reference and the sisters were saved from deportation and allowed to remain in their home. Other people returned things left by my parents. Mother had entrusted Mr Daniel, the tailor, with several lengths of woollen fabrics. As I did not need all of it for myself, I gave some to Aunt Frieda and to my cousin Zsuzsi. I kept a bolt of blue material for myself and Mr Daniel styled it into a lovely coat for me. Another navy pinstriped length was made into a new suit. All of this helped my transition into a new life.

Aunt Irene in Palestine responded to a letter I had sent earlier and she sent parcels of clothing and money. Life had resumed, and I was slowly rebuilding my life. A relative of Aunt Irene, Mathew, was a young soldier who had served in the Czechoslovakian Brigade and was stationed in Italy. He sent crates of oranges and rice. We shared these wonderful things among the family and I sent some to Bozena in Pilzen. I re-established contact with former school friends, Greta, Ilse and Eva. We were all orphans so we had a lot in common. We formed a close bond and spent a good deal of time together.

The Jewish High Holy Days brought us great sadness. We attended the first memorial service, *Yiskor*, in the Heyduk Synagogue. My heart broke as the prayers were recited and the memories of the war years returned. Tears streamed down my face and sobs heaved from deep within. It was too much. I fled the shul and wanted to disappear from the face of the earth. The healing would take a long time, and there are parts that will never heal.

However, physically I was on the mend. My feet were slowly recovering although I had to bandage them every night to try and get the swelling down. My hair was growing back, darker than before, but nice and curly. I still felt ugly, but with my new kimono-sleeved coat and the shoes Aunt Irene had sent me, I had more confidence and began to go out for walks. Together with friends, I walked along the banks of the Danube and through the once beautiful parts of the city. I couldn't totally enjoy the natural beauty I saw about me because there had been too much pain connected with this city. I had walked these streets with my parents and sister years before, and even though I was now with friends, in many ways I walked alone, always alone. It was only the love of Aunt Frieda and Uncle Ernie and their family that kept me from despairing altogether. They were wonderful people and a great support when I needed it most.

Another surprise occurred when Hugo Grossmann, the young man I had met in the camp at Sered, turned up to visit me. He had promised he would return and look me up. Well, I was certainly not the attractive young girl he remembered from the summer of 1944. He must have gotten such a shock when he saw me because he vanished and I never saw or heard of him again.

I travelled to Cifer and Sala to see what happened to my parent's property and my grandmother's house. Cifer was a terrible disappointment, and Sala was a nightmare. The Kramars who leased the Cifer property from my parents told me bluntly that the property was no longer mine since they purchased it under the previous Slovakian regime. They had been convinced that we were all dead and no one would ever return to claim the estate so it was now theirs. I left ...

The train trip to Sala filled me with memories of the happy days spent with my grandmother. When I reached the house I barely recognised it. The garden where I had played as a child and which Grandmother had so carefully tended was overrun and wild. The house looked as though it had been bombed. Anything of any value had been looted. Window frames and doors had been taken. The front entrance was blocked with debris and human faeces. I couldn't even get inside. Human waste from the village had been dumped throughout the property. Nothing was left but a gutted shell. I learnt that the house had been ransacked after my grandmother was deported. A Jewish house was always 'fair game'. I felt as though every aspect of my life before the war was gone, destroyed by anti-semitism, hatred and greed. I turned around, walked to the railway station and took the next train home.

I wanted to go back to school and finish my education. It had been over four years since I had sat in a classroom. I was refused permission because previously I had been a student in a German language school! My friend Greta also tried. She sat for the examinations twice and was failed twice. It was becoming clear that there was nothing left for me in Bratislava. All that I had treasured was gone. For me, there was no future in Czechoslovakia. I began making plans to go to Palestine. However, that required money and so I had to get a job.

The owner of an interior-decorating business offered me a part-time job with his firm. It was only for a few hours a day with only a small wage, but it was a job, and the money came in handy for buying the things I needed. My confidence began to return but the manager, a married man, took an unhealthy interest in me. He would often make suggestive advances and I felt uncomfortable and scared. I had to ask the other women who worked there not to leave the shop so that I wouldn't be left alone with him.

Once I started work, I began planning the trip to Palestine. I went to the Zionist office in Bratislava and made enquiries. Proxy marriages were arranged with single returned soldiers from the Czechoslovakian Brigade who had 'brides' written into their passports before they returned to Palestine. I thought this was a good idea and I saw myself joining a Kibbutz and building a new life in the Promised Land. I had put on weight, my hair had grown back and I felt I looked better, but my body was still far from recovered. Aunt Frieda was concerned enough to urge me to see a doctor though I dreaded doing so. I still had visions of the 'Angel of Death' at Auschwitz, Mengele, and so I would not see or consult, much less undress in front of any doctor. I put up with the condition and waited for my body to heal itself.

In the meantime, something else happened that was to change my life. After the war, people searched across Europe for their family and loved ones. Many were bitterly crushed to find that they were the only survivors. One young man in this situation was Micki, the brother of my girlfriend Gerti. He had joined the British army in Palestine and was later in the Royal Navy – the only Jewish officer in the fleet. He was a qualified electronics engineer. He arrived in Bratislava still wearing the impressive, starched white naval uniform and we all planned to go to the annual medical ball. I was excited! This was to be my first 'formal' outing.

Greta and I busied ourselves designing and making our formal ballgowns – hers yellow tulle and mine pink. The dresses turned out to be very pretty and we were delighted with our handiwork. My cousin Zsuzsi and her husband Jeno were our chaperones. The evening was held in the ballroom of the old and impressive Redoute building. It was the first 'formal' since the end of the war. All the men wore evening dress and the women, long formal ball-gowns. The Ballroom was beautifully decorated. There was an orchestra and the atmosphere was very romantic. Young men came and bowed and asked me to dance. I don't know how I managed! I'd never danced before and was still shaky on my feet. Zsuzsi started plotting and arranging a meeting between me and the brother of her friend Edith. I was not impressed and rejected the idea. However, I hadn't counted on the man concerned being so blunt as to ring me and invite me out. Which is exactly what happened.

Some days later the telephone rang and John Horak, Edith's brother, invited me to a soccer game. John was a polite and mature young man. He had survived the war in hiding under dangerous circumstances. He had a good sense of humour and he made me laugh.

John had a cousin, Otto, who had developed a bad toothache. John invited him to join our group for dinner one day, enjoy the company and forget about his tooth. Otto came along and did more than forget about his tooth. He met Greta, struck up a friendship and fell in love. After a three-month courtship they were married and have remained deeply in love since. They were a terrific match and theirs has been a very happy union. In ways such as this we were similar to many other young survivors who lost everyone. We wanted to establish ourselves, marry and begin a new family.

John and I were now very much attracted to each other and finally, he 'popped the question'. I accepted his proposal and after a formal six-month courtship we were engaged on 15 September 1946. John and I married on 9 February 1947. I was so very happy. Our wedding took place in the Hayduk synagogue. Even though the shul looked poor – the Chuppah (marriage canopy) was neglected and undecorated – that was not going to diminish the joy that filled us both. My wedding dress was my navy blue pinstriped suit, a pale blue silk blouse with an Ascot tie, and a small matching pale blue hat decorated with a bunch of silk violets. I carried a bouquet of six white lilies. In front of the Chuppah was an old chair and on it was the Kiddush wine and a glass. Our modest religious ceremony was followed by a cocktail reception party in the Savoy Hotel in the centre of Bratislava. From there John and I honeymooned in the Tatra mountains.

CHAPTER TEN

Australia

I WAS BORN again the day I was married to John Horak. John is also a Holocaust survivor. He was not deported but survived by hiding and being on the run throughout the war. When he returned home, he joined his brothers in the family business. He was determined to leave the country and start a new life, far away from Europe. With only modest, newly acquired assets, nothing would prevent him planning the escape to freedom.

Owing to the political changes in Czechoslovakia, it was difficult to obtain passports and only government officials were able to travel to different countries in the western zones. Under strict secrecy, contacts had to be established and finally we were the lucky holders of valid passports and issued with Swiss tourist visas as well. Now the planning began. John knew a border guard whom he approached and eventually convinced him to help us. He told us the exact time of his duty at the border. It was a very dangerous appointment but we took the risk. It was early in June 1948 when, late one evening, we locked the house and headed for the railway station to board a train to Budapest, Hungary.

We arrived at the border in the middle of the night. As soon as the train stopped, border guards approached and surrounded all the carriages. They came into the compartments to inspect documents and luggage. We were scared and nervous but relieved to see the guard who was our friendly contact. However, we had no idea what to expect. Our friendly man was in charge over the more junior guards and he commanded them to move on to other compartments and he himself would examine our passports and take care of the rest. He quickly messed up the contents of our open suitcases, embraced us, shook our hands and with tears in his eyes wished us the best of luck and good fortune. It was a very emotional moment, but now we knew we were on our way.

We crossed the border and a few hours later arrived in Budapest, where we stayed for one day before we resumed our trip to Vienna, Austria. We stayed in Vienna for one day and once again boarded a train to continue our escape to Switzerland. Finally we arrived in Zürich, totally exhausted, and were met by John's sister, her husband and their little boy Peter. They had escaped three weeks before us and now we happily joined them in exile.

After only a fortnight, when our tourist visa expired, we encountered problems. Again and again we had to explain that we wanted to stay in Switzerland until we were issued with documents enabling us to emigrate to America or Canada. We did not realise at the time that this was a hopeless plan as both countries had four to five years waiting lists for Czechoslovak nationals.

Switzerland is a beautiful country but we were not tourists, therefore our stay there was not very pleasant. We had limited funds, and they would not last us long. We were not allowed to work, and we could only stay if we could prove we had money in the bank. However, we made some good friends during our ten-month stay and were sad when we had to leave them behind.

After nearly a year in Zürich, we decided to make a move. John's sister, with her family, had already made arrangements to immigrate to Australia. We, too, longed finally to go to a new home. We did not know much about this 'far away Australia'. Of course we heard about kangaroos and learned in school about merino sheep, and the abundant sunshine and tropical weather conditions, but not much more. It was a challenge but we were ready to give it a go. We contacted my cousin in Melbourne and asked for his help, which he readily extended. We were a young, happily married couple and nothing could have spoilt our spirits. Preparing for this long voyage kept us busy for many weeks. We had just enough money left to purchase our tickets for our adventurous trip aboard a Greek ship. With mixed feelings, we left Zürich in August 1949 for Italy, and in Genoa we boarded the Greek liner *Cyrenia*.

Cyrenia was an old rust-bucket but seaworthy. The ship was overcrowded with migrants from different European countries. They, like us, hoped to start a new life far away. It was a very hot summer, and the ship had no air-conditioning nor a stabiliser. It was certainly not a luxury liner. The heat became intense and unbearable, especially when we passed through the Suez Canal. Flies and mosquitoes were in abundance. On board the ship the conditions were generally not bad, although there was a shortage of space. Most of the passengers were seasick and the smell in the small cabins was foul and rancid. I, too, was seasick but John was stronger and he came through with flying colours.

We reached Fremantle, Australia after having been at sea for thirty-two days. We were excited having finally arrived at our new homeland. We were keen to go ashore and with a few newly acquired friends, we took a train to Perth. I was convinced that I would be able to speak and also understand English but, to my disappointment, it was not as easy as I anticipated. Australian English was difficult to understand. It seemed to be different from the kind of English I had been taught. Often, I had to lip-read in order to get a message right. We had only a few hours in Perth and, from Fremantle port, left for Melbourne, the last port of call.

Cyrenia sailed into Melbourne on 16 September 1949 with a tired and anxious load of migrants. I saw luggage and boxes tied with strings being brought up from the ship's hold, hoisted with a crane. Some of the luggage dropped into the water and could not be salvaged. It was a pitiful sight as the helpless bystanders watched. The weather was already mild since it was springtime and the sun was shining. My cousin Max waited at the wharf to welcome us. We had come from the shores of the Danube across the sea to Australia. After spending two days in Melbourne with family, we took a night train to Sydney. Here, we were reunited with John's sister, her husband and little Peter, whom we loved so much.

Life in Australia was so very different and we had to adapt ourselves accordingly. Things which seemed strange at first soon became part of our lives. We tried hard to blend in and not to stand out because we looked and behaved differently from the Australians. We 'New Australians' shook hands. That was good manners in Europe but did not seem right here. Australians have the most immaculate table manners. European men did not part their hair. Australian men mostly wore Fairisle knitted cardigans and felt hats with their parted hairdos. People were mostly friendly, and conversations in buses or on trams took place among strangers and women often knitted diligently whilst travelling to their destination. So many things and so many ways were strange to us. We realised that even the moon shone from a different angle in the sky. We appreciated the beautiful climate and we did not mind the hot weather at all. We admired the green gardens with so many exotic flowers we had never seen before. We admired the majestic Harbour Bridge and we loved going to the beautiful beaches, soaked in the sunshine which was free for everyone.

As there was a great shortage of apartments, it was difficult to find the right place to move into. For a short while we shared a semi-detached house but it became too crowded and we all moved into separate flats. We were also concerned and anxious to start any sort of a business. Before we left Zürich, I bought a small collapsible 'Baby Singer' sewing machine with the thought that it might come in handy one day and indeed it did. As a young girl I learned how to sew, but I was never a qualified dressmaker nor was I trained for any other job. But I was a great improviser, and I had a flair for fashion and I loved designing clothes. I could not sew a full dress or anything more complicated. Therefore, we decided to start manufacturing ladies blouses. I was sure I would be able to make the upper part of a garment successfully.

York Street in the city was the centre for textiles. Our brother-in-law, who became our business partner, went with John to search for suitable fabrics. From ten different lengths of lovely silk and cotton materials, ten different designs of the latest styles of blouses were born. We had no workshop yet so I spread the fabrics on the bare floorboards in the lounge room, took a pair of very large scissors and ruthlessly, and without a paper pattern, cut into the nice fabrics. I taught myself how to make paper patterns and I had to make sure that the fit of the blouses was perfect as well. So a business was born. My husband loved being in the textile industry again. Our brother-in-law and John were the managers and I was the designer. Two weeks after our arrival in Sydney we established a business which we conducted for the next twenty-two years. We rented premises and with the expertise of my husband, who is a textile engineer, a proper factory was put together. We had lots of orders to execute and John looked after the production in a professional manner which resulted in us having a good reputation and satisfied customers. A few years later, we acquired the property and rebuilt it into the most modern factory building.

Our first daughter was born in 1950. After a long, hard labour, I looked at my beautiful little baby. I held her close and I felt the most blessed mother in this world. I had to get a babysitter to look after my girl as I could not stay away from work for too long. The babysitter was a very big, wonderful, warmhearted, Australian lady. She was reliable and she loved our baby, who later called her auntie. She was our adopted family member. We bought our own house and finally had our home with an established family. John studied English with a young university student and I tried to improve my English by reading. Our household was different in many ways from Australian households. The dialogue was different as well. There were no grandmas, grandpas or other family members. This was a matter which would be hard to explain to our children later on. Our second daughter was born in 1957 and again I was filled with happiness. To become a mother again was the ultimate blessing.

When the children were at school, I made sure that they were in a happy environment. They wore their school uniforms, with straw hats and gloves, and they looked so very cute with their bowties under the round starched collars. I learned how to make their school lunches. I learned how to make Australian sandwiches from white cottonwool-like square bread, spread with Vegemite, peanut butter or using hundreds and thousands to create fairy bread. Meanwhile we continued to work diligently in the factory, and our merchandise became well known and popular. This was the result of hard and consistent work and the love my husband John had for the factory he had built.

I had always felt the need to express myself through art and, now my children were at school, I enrolled at the

East Sydney Technical College. However, I could not join as they were booked out, but I was offered a second choice of attending to study sculpting with well-known Australian sculptor Lyndon Dadswell. I was hooked. I loved it and I finished the course after five years. Later I joined painting classes in the studio of John Ogburn, a very gifted Sydney artist, who was an inspiring and encouraging teacher. To my surprise I found myself sculpting elongated, skinny, skeleton-like figures and when painting flowers, they suddenly turned into skulls painted on black backgrounds. My inner feelings are affected by my tragic memories which are reflected in my artwork.

In 1995 the world celebrated the fiftieth jubilee of the end of World War II. Holocaust survivors, now spread all over the world, celebrated too, not only the end of the war but also 'liberation'. It remains a fact that we could not share in the happiness of this historic jubilee to the full, because, to most survivors, liberation came too late. I was asked to participate in Sydney. John Saunders AO, the benefactor of the Sydney Jewish Museum, arranged the most magnificent fiftieth jubilee celebration in the Sydney Opera House, on 7 May 1995. I found myself overcome by emotion when I stood on the huge stage giving a short testimony and expressing my thanks to my liberators. Representatives from overseas were invited as guests of honour; from Britain, the Hon. Lord Howe; from the United States, General Alexander Haig; from Russia, Dr Aleksandr Bessmertnykh and for Australia's involvement in the Liberation, Major General Paul Cullen, they all delivered unforgettable, emotional speeches. It was a most memorable evening indeed.

I am proud of having retained my identity and also my religious beliefs and traditions. I feel good being a volunteer guide and an active member at the Sydney Jewish Museum, but I still feel the hurt inflicted upon me and carry scars deep inside me. However, I would like to stress that I do not carry hatred within me. Hatred is ugly and brought on the most terrible tragedy in the twentieth century.

Whilst I am writing this last chapter, sitting at the desk, I am looking out the window. I can see sunshine and I can see the blue sky and I realise how lucky I am. I have been given a chance to live and for that I am grateful to our Lord the Almighty.

Appendix I

Family History

THE WEISS FAMILY
(Mother's Family Tree)

Ignacz **Weiss**　　*m*　　Ilona Friedlieb

Aranka　　*m*　　Dr Jakob **Weiss**
Fritz, Erwin, Thomas

Serena　　*m*　　Lipot **Haas**
Andrew, Leslie, Esther

Piroska (1905-1945)　　*m*　　1924 Hugo **Rosenberger** (1894-1944)
Judith (1925-1942), Olga (1926-)

Irene (?-1988)　　*m*　　Karl Roth (?-1989)
Miriam, Dita, Eva, Zwi (emigrated to Palestine 1939) (1948-)

Tivadar　　*m*　　Klara Fürst
Egon, Leslie

Nelly　　*m*　　Josef Holzer
Aniko

Ignacz and Ilona Weiss, my maternal grandparents, lived in Sala nad Va'hom, a small town on the Vah river not far to the south-east of Bratislava. The family had a well-established retail business and sold haberdashery, manchester and ready-to-wear ladies and gentlemen's garments. Ignacz and Ilona had six children: five daughters (Aranka, Serena, Piroska, Irene and Nelly) and one son (Tivadar). My mother, Piroska, was born on 12 February 1905.

The family house stood in the town square, an imposing building surrounded by trees and a well-tended garden. Fruit and berry trees gave the garden the appearance of a park. Paths lined with chestnut trees and grape trellis led towards Lake Poshvan towards the far end of the property. The Weiss house had seven large rooms, all facing and opening to a surrounding verandah. Along with the apartments for the family, there were two kitchens, the bathroom and quarters for a maid.

Ignacz died at a comparatively young age during an operation in Vienna. Ilona was left to carry on the family business. An energetic and intelligent woman, grandmother showed a considerable business skill. She bought properties and built a credit-banking house, which she managed with the help of her only son, Tivadar.

During the summer holidays most of the family went to Sala, to join Ilona. The house was alive with warmth and the happy atmosphere of children's laughter. Grandmother made sure that her children would be well educated. She arranged for them to board in Bratislava while attending high school. This was, in part, preparation for her daughters' eventual arranged marriages, still customary in the early twentieth century. It was important that spouses be found from suitable families of the appropriate class and social background. Introductions were made to young men considered suitable by Grandmother, who also ensured her daughters had adequate dowries. Aranka, the eldest daughter, married Dr Jakob Weiss, followed by Serena who married Lipot Haas, Piroska married Hugo Rosenberger, Irene who married Karl Roth, and Nelly who married Josef Holzer. Aranka, Piroska and Irene moved to Bratislava, while Serena and Nelly settled in Hungary after the weddings. All the sisters made frequent visits to the family home in Sala, often leaving the growing number of grandchildren with Ilona while they went with their husbands to holiday resorts for some of the vacation time. Grandmother supervised the children with the help of live-in nannies.

Tivadar, as the only son, was destined to inherit the family business, and was not to marry for some time. He travelled widely around the world taking his camera with him. When he returned from one of his trips, film nights in Grandmother's home were organised and friends and local children were invited to watch the recordings. The favourite films were those Tivadar took in Palestine in the early 1930s. However, Charlie Chaplin proved to be another great favourite on these nights as well. Tivadar eventually settled down and married Klara Fürst, and together they had two sons, Egon and Leslie. Tivadar and his family lived with Ilona in the family home in Sala.

In 1923 Hugo Rosenberger accompanied his brother

on a business trip to Sala. They were invited to dinner at the Weiss home. According to family lore, as he walked through the magnificent gardens towards the house, Hugo remarked, 'If the girls in the house are as beautiful as the garden, I will marry one of them!' That evening he met Piroska, and a year later they were married, making their home in Bratislava.

After Piroska's marriage, she too returned to Bratislava, so that there were three sisters in the city – Aranka, Piroska and Irene, who later married Karl Roth. The sisters were very close and used their own secret language when they chatted for hours on the telephone. No one could understand what they said since they spoke very quickly.

Each of Ilona's daughters received 250 000 crowns as part of her dowry. Piroska invested her share in fifty hectares of prime land in Cifer, near Trnava, a town about thirty kilometres north of Bratislava. The property was leased to a local Slovakian family, the Kramars. Every year at harvest time they brought bags of flour to us. This was followed by a great celebration during which the Kramar family dressed in exquisitely embroidered Slovak national dress, and the daughter Maria Kramar sang local folk songs in her rich and resonant voice.

Our relations with the Kramars were good. In the late 1930s Maria went to Bratislava to study singing. She fell in love with a postal clerk and soon there was a baby on the way. They wanted to get married and we were invited to the wedding. My father drove us in his Tatra convertible. Maria wore a magnificently rich embroidered national costume and her already large tummy was amply covered with a fully gathered embroidered apron. The village priest celebrated the wedding and the young couple started their married life together. Soon afterwards, Maria gave birth to a healthy baby boy. The fact that we felt comfortable going to a Catholic wedding celebration and that the Kramars were happy to have us there went beyond our professional relationship. It was a case of friendship. And in hindsight, I believe it was a rare and treasured moment we shared with them.

Grandmother Ilona lived in Sala with her son and his family until 1944. Their beautiful family life ended when the Hungarian Nazis raided the house one Friday evening when the family was eating dinner. While the Sabbath candles burned on the table, the fascists ransacked and looted the house before arresting the family. None survived the war.

Of my maternal family, only my Aunt Irene and her family escaped the Holocaust. In 1939, Irene and Karl with their three daughters – Miriam, Dita and Eva – immigrated to Palestine. A son Zwi was born in 1948 in Tel Aviv. Irene died in 1988, followed by her husband in 1989. The only other close member of the Weiss family known to have survived was a niece of Ilona's, Erika Blumgrund (nee Friedlieb) who lives with her family in Buenos Aires, Argentina. I have other relatives who live in Canada.

THE ROSENBERGER FAMILY

(Father's Family Tree)

Markus Rosenberger *m* Maria Neumann

Adolf *m* Jolanda Baer
—————————————————
Rozsi, Alexander, Edith, Hedi, Marcel

Sigmund *m* Rosa Fischer
—————————————————
Zoltan, Violetta, Gerti, Paul

Julius *m* Martha Neumann
—————————————————
Max, Eva

Frieda *m* Oskar Nachmias
—————————————————
Alexander, Renee, Eugene, Arpad

William *m* Jolanda Kaltmann
—————————————————
Erika, Herta, Magda

Hugo *m* Piroska Weiss
—————————————————
Judith, Olga

David *m* Franziska Menczer
—————————————————
Ruth, Marcel

Selma *m* Bibi Moses Stern
—————————————————
Max, Trude, Lilly, Kurt, Harry, Jossie, Robbie

(All members of the family lived in Bratislava)

Markus and Maria Rosenberger lived in Bratislava, the capital of Slovakia. Maria was born in Podivin (Kostl) in Moravia, and was known in the family as Marie Omama. My father, Hugo, was born 13 April 1894, the fifth son and sixth child of my grandparents. He was surrounded by his older brothers, Adolf, Sigmund, William, twins Julius and Frieda, and his younger brother and sister, David and Selma.

The Rosenberger's were well known in the cattle business. Grandfather Rosenberger was a successful breeder of cattle and established his own farm, Majerhof, about ten kilometres outside the city, in the suburb of Ruzinov (Rosenheim). Although the property was a dairy farm, it was mainly used for breeding stud for livestock. A manager who lived there with his wife and child in a small comfortable cottage that had a pretty flower-filled garden out the front, cared for the 1000 hectare farm. Watermelons, rockmelons and sugarbeet grew in the fields as fodder. Adolf, William and David joined their father in the cattle trade. Sigmund married Rosa Fischer and went on to manage his father-in-law's wholesale textile business. Hugo, my father, was apprenticed to a local brewery, where he eventually became a junior executive manager. He returned to the family business after the untimely death of Grandfather, shortly before he was to be married.

The farm produced some of the best cattle in central Europe winning the family hundreds of first prize awards at the annual agricultural exhibition. After the death of Grandfather, the business was formed into a company with my father and my uncles Adolf, William and David as directors. Julius was the 'black sheep' of the family. He loved gambling and neglected his wife Martha and children, Max and Eva. Omama and my uncles looked after Julius' family providing the care that their husband and father appeared unable to do.

My grandfather was a devout man who worked to ensure that his fellow Jews were able to observe the *Mitzvot* when outside Jewish environments. An example of this was his work to help provide a kosher kitchen for observant Jewish patients in the new State Hospital built in Bratislava in 1890. A kosher kitchen was established and supervised by a team of dieticians and medical staff. Within a short time other hospitals recognised similar needs for their Jewish patients and a committee of 800 financial members was founded together with the *Chevra Kadisha*. My grandfather was among those who received the highest accolades from the management and directors of the Bratislava Hospital.

My grandparent's home was a large house that stretched over two blocks of land between Miczkiewicova Ulica 16 and Spitalska Ulica 45. Basement rooms eventually became an air-raid shelter. The house also had the only council-tolerated stables in Bratislava. These were kept for the showcattle, which were brought to the city and kept there during transit to other locations. The stables were four whitewashed halls with hot and cold running water. They were kept clean by the two white-uniformed servants.

My grandmother Rosenberger was a great 'grand lady', respected by her children and by the people of Bratislava. She was very beautiful: fair, blue-eyed, tall and slim. Deeply religious, Omama wore a wig that greyed with the passing of time. Always well groomed, my very proud grandmother wore a velvet choker studded with little pearls and trimmed with lace in order to cover her wrinkled throat. Her dresses were mostly black or grey with little printed patterns all carefully tailored. As she grew older she would sometimes add a little padding to give her a better shape. Even in old age, my grandmother walked fully upright and her mind was clear as crystal.

After the death of my grandfather, Omama presided over the family. Every Sabbath afternoon all her children and some of her twenty-nine grandchildren came to visit her. We all lined up to kiss her hand. We loved and adored our Omama! Omama was known throughout the city for her charity. She freely distributed food to the poor who came to the house on different days of the week. Milk from the family farm was sent to hospitals and orphanages. However, Omama was not one to hide away! She regularly chatted with the stableboys, enquired about calving and spoke business with the farm manager. Her sons often sought her business advice and it was readily accepted. My beloved Omama was close to eighty when the Nazis came for her. She went with her family on the trains to Auschwitz. She never came home.

HUGO AND PIROSKA ROSENBERGER
After my parent's married, they lived in Bratislava in a rented apartment in Spitalgasse 50 (Hospital Street). Their first child, my sister, Judith, was born on 12 April 1925. I followed on 11 August 1926, barely sixteen months later. We had a live-in nanny, Marcelle, who was responsible

for the care of Judith and me. My parents also had a maid who took care of the daily running of the household. Some time after this, we moved into the family house in Miczkiewicova Ulica 16/Spitalska Ulica 45. Omama lived on the ground floor of the same house. Our apartment was large with rooms inter-connected with shiny white lacquered French doors. I remember only a little of my childhood years. My sister Judith, being the first born child, was, as was the custom then, given the first rights in everything. We looked like twins. We were the same height and size and wore identical clothing. Judith had shiny brown hair that was straight, hazel eyes, a round face and lovely pink cheeks. I had fair curly blond hair, hazel eyes, a thin face and a pale complexion. I was a frail little girl and I managed to pick up all sorts of illnesses. Together with my sister we had whooping cough, and I remember our nanny taking us for long walks near the gas factory to inhale the air which lingered around the huge gas containers. This was meant to be good for us.

My mother saw her sisters almost every day. This formed the most important part of her social life. She seldom visited coffeehouses and never played cards. These things were not considered appropriate for a woman of her social standing. Mother was an intelligent and well-read lady who borrowed books frequently from the local library. She also belonged to the local WIZO group and regularly attended their meetings.

My memories of my father are quite distinct. He was the most gentle, kind person, and I simply adored him. I was daddy's little girl. Often, I would walk into his office and sit on his lap, paper and pencil in hand, ready to draw his portrait. And he would proudly show his daughter's artistry to everyone near him! Tall and slim, Father had blue-grey eyes, short-cropped blond hair with a well-trimmed moustache and he wore frameless glasses. Like my mother, Father was always well dressed. For going out on Saturdays he wore a furlined coat. For work he wore a fur hat, and lambswool lined boots. This was because there was no heating in the car and it could get very cold. My mother had a coat tailored from black shiny broadtail pelts.

A wonderful sense of humour followed him everywhere. For my Omama, he was a loyal and devoted son; for my mother he was a loving husband and dedicated father. It is this picture of the man I remember so well. A modern man at home with the early twentieth century. My father loved and valued his Judaism. Every Friday night after he returned from shul, he would bless Judith and myself. I can still hear him recite the berecha, 'Jevo-rachacho-vejishmerecho.' I remember too that Omama spent every Sabbath with us. She often brought her own double toasted pieces of bread with her, which kept us children curious. She also touched all freshly baked cheese pockets before she decided which one to take. Now, I understand what she was doing. She needed to have a soft cake that was easy on her dentures.

Father was an early riser and a heavy smoker, and would take great pleasure in driving his grey Tatra convertible out to Majerhof to supervise the milking of about 500 cows. Then he would discuss the daily agenda with the manager. He would then meet with the veterinarian as the livestock had to be constantly treated and supervised during calving. Only the best livestock was kept in the stables for breeding. They were exhibited at the animal fair, *Donaumesse,* and many ribbons were awarded for First Prize. Prize-winning cattle were then exported to Switzerland, Holland and Denmark. I remember two local butchers, Manderla and Kysely were customers who had been associated with my father and his brothers for many years. Rosenberger beef was highly sought after for the tables of Bratislava. My father was respected by his employees for being a good-hearted, honourable and charitable employer.

Business meant that my father travelled widely throughout Europe. Once, when returning from Paris, he realised he had forgotten to buy my mother a present. On his way home from the railway station, he saw a crocodile handbag in the window of an elegant leatherware shop. Quickly purchasing it, he didn't notice that it had faded from being exposed in the shop window. Father may not have noticed it, but mother did! Father confessed that the bag was a local product, not a gift from one of the fine salons in Paris. Mother forgave him at once, and eventually had the bag exchanged for one that looked a little more chic!

When Uncle Adolf and his family moved from the old house to another part of the city, my parents did not hesitate to move into the newly vacated first floor above Omama. Mother decided to have the whole place renovated. Rooms were made large and bright. The bathroom was modern and roomy; a feature was the recessed toilet and bidet. All rooms had beautiful ceramic-tiled fireplaces and parquet floors.

Judith and I shared a room. It was pretty and specially furnished for us in the new home. As we grew up we needed larger wardrobes and instead of the tubular chrome beds, we now had a large settee that turned into a double bed at night. This was very practical. Our room looked happy, the furniture painted in high gloss pale yellow with a rust coloured trim as a contrast.

My parent's bedroom looked very pretty indeed. It was of a pale cherrywood, carefully carved with small roses on top of the wardrobes and the top of the bed ends. In front of the bed was a chaise lounge covered with a soft silk Persian rug.

The dining room was formal. Furniture was made from dark brown palisander timber – a majestic curved sideboard, display cabinets and an impressive large oval table with silk damask covered chairs. The table was also covered with a silk Persian rug and above the table suspended from the ceiling was a solid silver bell. Ornaments and paintings completed the decoration in this room.

Father's study was equally wonderful. His furniture was carved from ebony timber. A crimson-velvet settee and two matching armchairs with a coffee table sat in the study. In the corner was a large writing desk and chair, against the wall a tall bookcase with glass doors allowing him to see the large leather bound volumes. It was from this case my father would take his volumes of the Talmud for study oneg shabbat. I grew up in a home filled with warmth, love and happiness.

EDUCATION AND SCHOOL

My sister and I started school in Bratislava's German-speaking Jewish primary school. After five years there, we were booked into two different high schools. One was the Slovak-speaking Gymnasium, and the other an exclusive German-speaking special high school for girls, the Zivnodom. Both of us passed the entry examinations for both schools and it was then decided that we would both go to the Zivnodom. We were kept under strict discipline. We didn't wear uniforms, but it was accepted that we wore navy blue box-pleated skirts with matching blouses and sailor collars trimmed with white braid.

The Zivnodom occupied three floors in a large private building. It was modern and elevators brought us to the respective floors. We had to remove our shoes and slip into special soft slippers, as the floor was a beautiful pale coloured parquetry. Our teachers were strict, and all of them were professors. My class teacher was an elderly, kind lady, Frau Kessler. I remember having Fraulein Ulrich for maths. I was good at school and found I didn't have to study too hard. A good memory got me through most of my homework subjects without great hardship. Judith was also a good student who liked all her subjects except art. So I did her artwork for her, which I didn't mind at all! I loved art and so my parents sent me to receive private lessons from a well-known painter, Professor Reichenthal.

We studied home science, cooking in real kitchens with real food, typewriting and shorthand. Physical education was also very important. Since the school did not have its own exercise hall, we went twice a week to another high school and used their equipment.

Outside of school we were kept busy with Madam Kühmayer, our French tutor. Madame Kühmayer was from Alsace and the wife of a prominent sculptor. She spoke very limited German, so we had to speak to her in French. Judith and I would go for lessons in the Kühmayer apartment that was only a few minutes walk from home. They had no children, but had the cutest little pet monkey. We were amused to watch him sit at the dressing table imitating his 'mummy.' He would take a powder puff and powder his entire face! He was tiny, hardly a metre tall, and looked very human.

We learnt to speak well-crafted English from Mr White, an Oxford trained professor. For a time, we studied Hebrew at a course provided by a Zionist organisation. Then it was off to Magda Fenyves's dance studio for gymnastics and occasional visits to an orthopaedic surgeon's rooms where we used equipment that stretched us in order to improve our posture. Our days were very full indeed.

Exercise was a daily part of our routine. We often went swimming in the summer, and in winter we took part in ice-skating. The Grösslingbath was an under cover indoor swimming pool open throughout the year. For hygienic reasons, people had to shower in provided areas before entering the pool. The ice-skating rink, the Schiffbeckgarten, was across the road from where we lived. It was a big park and in the grounds were the medical faculty and tennis courts. We had skate blades that were adjusted to our winter lace-up shoes with simple screws around the outside of the shoes. Mother often joined us and enjoyed skating. Although we were members of the skating club we did not get lessons, but managed quite well in our own childish way.

Bratislava was a pretty city. Surrounded by hills and forests, people could go skiing to the Koliba without travelling to higher mountains or ski resorts. About ten kilometres from the city was the Zelezna Studienka (Eisenbrunnel), a national park. Our family would go on picnics there. We would hire canoes and my father taught us how to paddle and use the oars correctly. Sometimes we ate our packed lunch on the grass near the lake in the forest or in the open-air beergarden restaurant. We listened to folk music played by accordionists while we munched on salt sticks, korozot with chives and drank the local beer. People would dance the polka and mazurka giving the place an air of happiness and relaxation.

In the centre of the city was the Friedrichspark, a well-tended garden park. When we were little we would take our diabolo sticks and hoops to play there. The corso on the banks of the Danube was a fashionable place for walking and a popular meeting rendezvous. When Judith reached her twelfth birthday in 1937, my parents bought her a bicycle. It was a ladies *Wanderer*, black and chromeplated. This was her *bat mitzvah* present, which was also meant to be shared with me. Judith loved her bike and spent so much time on it that I rarely got a chance to ride it. This left me sad. Fortunately, my parents realised what had happened, so they bought a bicycle for me – a *bat mitzvah* present one year early! Grandmother Ilona gave each of us precious rings for our *bat mitzvah*, but we were not allowed to wear such expensive jewellery at our young age.

Holidays were mostly spent at Sala with my grand-mother Weiss. This gave our parents time to go to the resort towns such as Karlsbad, Marienbad, Luhacovice and Trenin Teplic, all famous for their healing spas. In some places people took hot mudbath treatments, in others they drank the curative waters to heal ulcers and digestive complaints. Luxury hotels catered for the needs of Europe's crowned heads as well as the rich and famous. Guests walked for hours through the parks, sipping the 'wonder water' through straws. The water worked its 'magic' quickly and toilets were erected in rows everywhere. My father often visited Joachimov (Joachimstal) because he suffered from rheumatism and there he was treated with uranium rich water in a pool.

We enjoyed our holidays at Sala with Grandmother Ilona. Grandmother's property held so many wonders for children. She bred pigeons and had a tall pigeon house built in the garden. Often we would see her climb the ladder to peer through the round ventilation holes to check on the hatchlings. We loved picking blackberries, although more berries ended up in our mouths and all over our faces than in the basket! At the far end of the garden was the lake. During winter it froze and we went ice-skating with the children from the local village. Among our friends in Sala were the children of the local notary, Dr Zimmer. They were a local Jewish family, all of whom perished.

Sala was also special for *Pessach*. The entire family gathered at Grandmother Ilona's to celebrate Passover. I vividly remember the special smell of chicken soup with the matzo dumplings, the layered matzo walnut cake and huge square sponge cakes with orange cream. Life was not dull for us children.

If it was to Grandmother Ilona we went for *Pessach*, it was at Omama's we gathered for *Sukkot*. Each year a wooden *sukkah* was built in the courtyard of the family's house. We decorated it with real apples, painted walnuts and other coloured ornaments suspended from the green leaf covered rafters off the ceiling. All the aunts tried to outdo one another when meals were consumed together in the sukkah. All fineries were shown and the best food served. My mother was a fine cook and, to use a very Australian expression 'competed with the best of them'.

One of the last pre-war celebrations I remember was the wedding of my cousin Rozsi Rosenberger in 1938. Judith and I were flower girls at the wedding ceremony. In September 1939 we listened with shock with the rest of Europe and the world at the news of the German invasion of Poland. We had seen the Anchluss in neighbouring Austria, and had witnessed the destruction of Czechoslovakia and the creation of the puppet-state under Monsignor Tiso. And yet to me it all seemed so far away.

Appendix II

A Brief History of Slovakia

The Bratislavian Coat of Arms

Slovakia lies in the centre of Europe. Its topographical and political geography in the 1990s bears great resemblance to the medieval kingdom, the Hapsburg province and the state of 1939. Bordered by Austria to the south-west, the Czech lands directly to the north-west, Poland to the north-east, and Hungary and Romania to the south, landlocked Slovakia sits at a major European crossroad. The Danube forms a natural border between Slovakia and Hungary; the Tatra and Carpathian Mountains divide her from Poland and Romania and the Morava and Vah rivers separate her from the Czech lands of Bohemia and Moravia.

Bratislava, Slovakia's capital city, stands on the Danube barely sixty kilometres from Vienna. An ancient city with roots extending back into Europe's Iron Age, with evidence of human settlement from up to ten thousand years ago. Many peoples settled around the area in a series of migrations that characterised central European settlements in pre-feudal times. Among these were the Celts who arrived between 500–100 BCE and the early Germanic tribes who together formed the local people at the time when the Danube formed the *Limes Romanum*, the frontier of the Empire. These same German tribes were driven out in the sixth century CE by Attila the Hun. Finally, between 500 and 700 CE, Slavonic people from east of the Vistula River put down roots and have formed the majority ethnic group ever since. They mixed with the Germanic and Magyar peoples who came later, together shaping an identifiable Bratislavan culture.

German and Frankish missionaries brought Christianity to the region in the eighth century and the famous Slavic saints Cyril and Methodius worked for a time around Bratislava. With the Church came greater western European influence and for a great part of the next three centuries Bratislava was under Bavarian rule. Polish sovereignty was also exercised over the area until Bratislava became part of the Hungarian Kingdom around 1200.

Its ideal location on the banks of the Danube meant that Bratislava grew as a trading town. Major social and economic reforms at the beginning of the thirteenth century opened Bratislava to western political, economic and cultural influences. To the town came craftspeople from across Europe. Italians, German speakers and Arabs established businesses in Bratislava. And among the traders and merchants there also came the Jews adding to the cosmopolitan mix of the region. Records of the town show it was a medium settlement with medium density housing, an uncharacteristic feature in Central Europe at that time. Gardens and vineyards surrounded the town on the slopes of the Little Carpathian Mountains.

Bratislava became a Hungarian royal town in the twelfth century and enjoyed privileges bestowed by the Holy Roman Empire, including mayor and town magistrates. Atop the hill was built a castle that served as a royal residence when the Emperor visited the city. At the beginning of the fifteenth century, Sigismund de Luxembourg, son of the Emperor Charles IV, demolished the old castle and built a magnificent gothic residence. Unfortunately, he died before it was completed. The palace became a landmark of Bratislava, which could be seen from the distance. Bratislava was also marked with a range of architectural styles within the town itself, not least of which were a series of gothic churches and a gothic synagogue.

Religious tensions over many years in the fifteenth century destabilised Bratislava and Slovakia so that by 1490 the region was in decline and under Polish rule. The onset of the Turks and the effects of the Reformation further exacerbated the decline. One long term feature of this time was the growth of Magyar influence as ethnic Christian Hungarians crossed from the Ottoman provinces into Slovakia. After the Hapsburgs reclaimed the territory, Slovakia began a long period of restoration.

Bratislava's greatest privilege was the dignity of being the city of coronation. Between 1563 and 1830, eleven Hapsburg monarchs, including the Empress Maria

Teresa, were crowned in the city. Traditionally Catholic, Bratislava was the only major Slovakian region that embraced the reformed religion of Martin Luther during the Reformation. This distinguished the urban centre from the predominantly Roman and Uniate Catholic rural districts of Slovakia. And this in turn became a cause for tensions that remained throughout the region's history until 1945. Protestants were mostly urban and engaged in town based occupations. This opened them up to contacts across the Austro-Hungarian Empire as well as into Western Europe. Catholics remained rural and politically and culturally inexperienced.

Jews arrived in significant numbers in Bratislava during the seventeenth century at the invitation of Count Palffi who re-established the community that had been driven from the town in the 1530s. The reason for the expulsion almost certainly came from Luther's failed hope that the Jews would convert to his reformed version of Christianity now that it was free from the evils of Roman Catholicism. There is no evidence to suggest that the new relationship between the Jews and Christians in the seventeenth century were anything other than cordial. As restrictions were lifted throughout the Hapsburg realms, Jews became more and more a part of local urban life. As with Jews elsewhere in Europe's cities, the Jews of Bratislava were engaged in a mix of professions mostly centred on commerce and trade.

Following the final defeat of the Turks in 1683, Central Europe enjoyed a period of great peace and prosperity. Bratislava entered its next stage of development. It was during the eighteenth century that Bratislava emerged as one of the showpieces of the Hapsburg baroque. Maria Teresa ordered much of the city rebuilt and significant numbers of the local aristocracy imitated Viennese styles in their town houses and the public buildings of the city. New suburbs encircled the town spreading out into the local countryside. The Empress had the gothic castle renovated in the Rococco style popular in the late eighteenth century. The castle remained a focal point for the city until it was destroyed by fire in 1811. It remained a ruin until 1950 when the Czechoslovak government undertook a restoration program. Today it houses the Slovak National Council and the Slovak National Museum.

Upon the Empress' death in 1780, the Hapsburgs moved the Imperial court to Buda. In 1848 the Parliament of Hungary was also moved to Buda. Industry now replaced the city's previous political and cultural importance. In 1840, the first rail link was made between Bratislava and Trnava, with the carriages drawn by horses. The advent of steam-powered trains linked the Danubian city with the rest of Europe and made Bratislava a major transit point for trade from the Balkans, Germany, Austria-Hungary and Russian Poland.

With the division of the Austro-Hungarian Empire in 1867 and the creation of the Dual Monarchy, the land of the Slovakians became part of Hungary and the policy of deliberate Magyarisation began in 1848 after the 'Year of Revolutions' continued. Hungary was determined to carve and create an ethnically homogenous state out of the Hapsburg domains. As many as 30 000 Slovakians emigrated. This pattern remained so until 1914.

Fighting as part of the Austro-Hungarian Empire during World War I, many in Slovakia hoped for independence from Hapsburgs and the creation of a Slovakian nation. Their hopes were dashed with the establishment of a Czecho-Slovak union that was given the blessing of the Allied Victors at the Paris Peace Conference in 1919. Leading the new state was a predominantly Czech administration that was loath to give full consideration to the aspirations of the Slovakian people.

CZECHOSLOVAKIA 1920–1938

Slovakia was absorbed into Czecho-Slovakia after a failed attempt to create an independent Slovak state in late 1918. This was in part due to Slovakia's political inexperience during the last decades of Hapsburg rule. When Austria-Hungary ceased to exist, the majority of the Hungarian civil servants left to return home. Quickly, Prague filled the vacuum with Czech administrators who had little understanding of Slovakian conditions or needs.

The democracy that was established in the new state was modelled on the United States of America. (The USA at the time was the most heterogeneous country in the world having just gone through the largest migration in history!) President Thomas Masaryk wanted to create one nation out of the many different groups within the country. Keeping the Slovaks mollified was vital for this. Together the Czechs and Slovaks accounted for sixty-five per cent of the population, with Germans, Hungarians, Ruthenians and Poles being accorded the status of 'national minorities'. The balance was precarious. Each 'minority' looked to their 'people' outside of Czecho-Slovakia and resented the new artificial state. Within the new state were approximately 356 830 Jews. 136 739 lived in Slovakia.

Throughout the 1920s Czecho-Slovakia, or Czechoslovakia as it became in 1921, enjoyed a domestic prosperity and political stability that was often the envy of other European countries. Under Masaryk's governments roads and railways were extended and improved. The country enjoyed progressive social legislation that protected the rights of workers, the sick, unemployed and retired. Education was a government priority and by the middle of the decade Czechoslovakia had one of the highest literacy rates and extensive education systems in the world. It was for reasons such as these that Czechoslovakia became known as a 'model democracy'.

The stability the country enjoyed in the 1920s ended with the onset of the Great Depression, 1930–1934. Coupled with the economic disaster was the emergence of a far more ominous threat from the north - The Third Reich. Konrad Henlein, leader of the *Sudeten Deutsche Partei* was encouraged by Berlin to create as much unrest as possible in order to embarrass Prague into granting more and more concessions. The long-term goal was, of course, annexation. The agreement made at Munich in September 1938 brought home the terrible truth for Czechs and Slovaks: the government was unable to protect the integrity of the state. Slovakian nationalists seized the opportunity to press for secession from the federation.

Less than a month after Munich, Prague granted

autonomy to a provincial Slovakian government led by Catholic priest, Dr Jozef Tiso. Tiso's first crisis was the question of Hungarian and Polish territorial demands on Slovakian land. Appealing to the new masters of Europe, Tiso pleaded for intervention to save Slovakia. Italy and Germany judged in favour of Hungary and Poland and ordered Tiso to surrender the disputed regions. Hungary took a large slice of southern Slovakia; Poland seized Tesin and part of Czech Silesia, while Germany annexed the Danube port town of Devin.

Democracy died in Slovakia after the November 1938 elections. Tiso dissolved all parties other than his Party of Slovakian National Unity and the Hlinka Slovak People's Party. Jews now had reason to fear. The Hlinka Guard was the most powerful organ of the HSPP and were notorious for their anti-semitism and the eagerness with which they sought out Jews for humiliation and beatings. Tiso's government was characterised by a balance preserved between the clerical fascism of Tiso and the more pro-Nazi group headed by Premier Tuka. The balance tilted in Tiso's favour for most of the time up to 1945.

The end of Czecho-Slovakia (as the country was renamed after Munich) was murky and desperate. Germany played a 'cat and mouse' game with Prague and Bratislava. Hitler at first indicated he was not interested in an independent Slovakia. Emil Hacha, the pressured Czech premier, ordered troops into Slovakia to prevent total secession. Tiso was dismissed on 10 March 1939 and Czech troops entered Slovakia the following day. Germany reacted by urging Tiso to declare independence or risk being handed over completely to Hungary. Tiso declared Slovakia fully

independent on 14 March. The next day Germany
annexed and occupied what remained of the rump
Czech state and renamed it the Reichsprotekorat of
Bohemia and Moravia.

SLOVAKIA 1939–1945

Confronting President Tiso in mid–March 1939 was a
serious dilemma. He favoured organising the state
according to the needs of the Slovakian. He was
particularly impressed by a model of Christian political
thought that was similar to the early model of Italian
corporate fascism. The alternative was to follow the
German example and imitate Hitler. Tiso's government
was divided between supporters of both models. These
tensions were to lead to devastating results, particularly
for the Jews of Slovakia.

There was no question of Slovakia not being an ally
of Germany. Slovakia depended upon German
investment in the country to support the economy. Tiso
attempted to maintain a façade of normality in the face
of Germany's hegemony over central Europe but his
country was in reality a 'puppet state' with a 'puppet
president'. Once the war broke out, Slovakia attempted
to remain neutral. Hitler rejected this position in July 1940.
Moderates were dismissed from Tiso's administration and
increasingly the links with Berlin grew stronger. The last
vestiges of independence ended in January 1941 after a
coup attempt failed to oust Tiso. Germany supported
Tiso who in turn publicly adopted the *Führerprinzip* as
his model of leadership. From October 1942 he titled
himself *Vodca* or Leader.

Tiso has been the subject of some debate since 1939. Was he a ruthless Slovakian Hitler or a cowed and malleable lackey? The truth is always somewhere in the middle ground. He had started out as a passionate Slovakian nationalist who mixed Catholicism and a brand of fascism together. He sincerely believed that Slovakia's future rested in it being as physically independent of Germany as possible without risking German interference. And to that end, Tiso ensured Slovakia had the highest European standard of living of any country between 1939–1944. However, all of this came at a cost. It suited Germany to have a compliant Slovakia and Hitler was willing to indulge Tiso's dreams of an independent Slovakia. Hitler also saw the sense in avoiding antagonising the Slovaks unnecessarily. Slovakia was a valuable source of middle industry, small arms and had a solid history of reliable economic and political stability. This was all in Germany's interests to maintain.

Tiso shared the anti-semitism of many of his co-religionists. 'Jews were too powerful in Slovakian society and needed to be restricted.' Throughout the rural districts of Slovakia, popular anti-semitism blended into the dominating Catholicism. The power and influence of the Catholic clergy over a largely peasant country was enormous. Often, the only literate person in the village, the parish priest was a de facto ruler of the area under his cure. Consequently, when the anti-Jewish Aktion started, centuries of superstition proved an excellent ally for the Nazis. Alongside superstition was old-fashioned greed at the prospect of gaining Jewish property and land.

SLOVAKIA AND THE 'FINAL SOLUTION'

Anti-Jewish measures were legislated in Slovakia in a half-hearted fashion during 1939. Strange pieces of law prohibiting Jews from participating in the manufacturing of Christian symbols of faith and defining who was and was not a Jew occupied legal minds. The comic aspect is overshadowed by the more sinister confiscation of Jewish rural land; the announcement of forced labour for all Jewish men between twenty and fifty years of age, and the *numerus clausus* of 18 April 1939. Under this law, Jews were restricted to four per cent of any profession. Fortunately, common sense over rode ideology. Forty-four per cent of Slovakia's doctors and thirty-six per cent of pharmacists were Jews. To apply the new restrictions would be ludicrous. However, the law had been created and set a dangerous precedent.

Restrictions increased in 1940. Jews were forbidden to own farms and Aryanization of Jewish business began in April. The most insidious laws were passed in September 1941. The *Codex Iudaicus* (The Jewish Code) was based on the 1935 Nuremberg Laws. In order to help Bratislava formulate the laws correctly, Berlin sent two advisers. One, *SS Sturmbannführer* Dieter Wisliczeny, was to return later to oversee the massive deportation process at the request of his superior officer, *SS Obersturmbannfürher* Adolf Eichmann. Jews were now forced to wear the yellow star and between 10 000 to 15 000 Jews were expelled from Bratislava.

Deportations for 'resettlement in the East' were ordered in October 1941. In July, a number of Slovak officials had visited several *Konzentrationslager* and Arbeitslager in Upper Silesia. The shock of what they saw was such that they put pressure on Tiso to insist that Germany promise to look after Slovakian Jews. To this end, Tiso promised to pay the German demand for RM500 per deportee to guarantee good treatment and cover 'resettlement' costs. Tiso's gesture of RM500 effectively covered the costs incurred by the *Reichsbahn* in transport, fed the guards and their dogs, maintained the tracks to the KL and helped defray the cost of purchasing Zyklon B. Of the 20 000 Jews deported in this first transport, some were sent to KL Auschwitz where they built the first gas chamber. The remainder were most likely murdered in Sobibor.

Further deportations took place between March and October 1942. The first transport was made up of 999 girls taken for 'work.' Breaking up families so upset Slovakian officials that a decision was made to expel whole families instead. This would relieve the emotional burden on relatives left behind! Keeping families together would also reduce the likelihood of escape. In the spring of 1942 around 7000 to 8000 Slovak Jews had fled into neighbouring Hungary. Among those who crossed the border were Hugo and Piroska Rosenberger and their youngest daughter Olga. Their older daughter Judith was among those taken in the first transport to Auschwitz.

Some 57 628 Jews were sent for 'resettlement'. Again, the vast majority were killed at Sobibor. Tiso's government rationalised the transports with the argument that under Article 22 of the *Codex*, Jews were obliged to work. Appeals from some Catholic Bishops, especially Bishop Kmetko of Nitra, and Lutheran clergy against the transports resulted in a halting of the trains in May and June. In April 1942 the government revised the *Codex* and gave Tiso the power to grant exemptions to deportation. Tiso did order a halt in transports in October claiming that Slovakia could deal with their 'Jewish Problem' in Slovakia. It appears that the Germans were not happy with this development but reasoned that they could wait for the time being.

Organised persecution lay primarily in Slovakian hands. Alexander Mach, the notoriously anti-semitic Minister of the Interior was head of both the Hlinka Guards and the secret police. No friend of the Jews, Mach was directly responsible for the implementation of anti-Jewish laws and for smooth-working with the 'Jewish advisers' from Berlin. Augustin Morávek headed the Central Economic Office that was responsible for Aryanization and the implementation of government anti-Jewish decrees. The CEO worked in conjunction with Anton Vasek's Department 14, a section of the Interior Ministry. This office ordered the work of expulsions and transports. Following the Nazi example of exploiting Jewish communal networks, Slovakia established the Jews' Centre that acted in a similar fashion to the Judenrat.

Slovakia remained relatively untouched by the war until the late summer of 1944. After the defeat of Stalingrad in January 1943 and the Allied landings in Italy later that year, many in Slovakia began to plan for the post-war years. As the Russians drew closer to the Carpathians and Romania looked set to leave the Axis, Slovakian partisan activity increased. A partisan led anti-

Tiso uprising was launched in September 1944. Tiso called for German assistance in suppressing the revolt. For two months the Germans fought the partisans before crushing the revolt. The price for Tiso was the loss of all vestiges of independence. Germany now ruled Slovakia directly and ordered the resumption of transports. Slovakia was to be made Judenrein before the arrival of the Red Army.

Eichmann was determined that the second round of Slovakian transports would not be interrupted as they had been in October 1942. He sent his able deputy, *SS Hauptsturmführer* Alois Brunner to supervise the deportations personally. Brunner lived up to his master's expectation. This time there were to be no exceptions, Brunner was determined to get every last Jew in Slovakia. From early 1944 until March 1945, eleven transports carrying 11 532 Jews were sent to Auschwitz. Among these was a young woman of sixteen – Olga Rosenberger.

Glossary

Arbeit Macht Frei	Work liberates
Arbeitslager	(German) Labour camp
Bat Mitzvah	(Hebrew) Religious celebration for Jewish girls when they reach the age of twelve
Berecha	(Hebrew) Blessing
Brausebad	(German) Bath house, also used to mean gas chamber
Brotkammer	(German) Bread chamber (or room) where bread was cut into slices before distribution to prisoners
Charasho	(Russian) All right
Chuppah	(Hebrew) Canopy under which a Jewish wedding is performed. It symbolises the wish for the newlyweds to have a roof over their heads
Davaj	(Russian) Give me
Donaumesse	(German) The Danube fair; an annual event in Bratislava
Ersatzkaffee	(German) Substitute coffee made from chicory
Frau	(German) Mrs
Fräulein	(German) Miss
Führerprinzip	(German) The theory of control by one leader

Herrenvolk	(German) Superior race
HSPP	(Slovak) Hlinkas Slovak People's Party
Hundertschaft	(German) Labour gang of 100 people
Judenrat	(German) Jewish administration advisory office for local affairs
Judenrein	(German) Free of Jews
Kapo	Camp prisoner placed in charge of other prisoners
Kashrut	(Hebrew) Jewish dietary law
KEOK	(Hungarian; abbreviation of Külföldieket Ellenörzök Orszagos Köszpontja) The central national security force to protect Hungary from foreigners (Jews)
Kindertransport	(German) Last-ditch attempts by Jewish families to send their children to safety, out of reach of the Nazis
KL	(abbreviation of Konzentrationslager) Concentration Camp
Konzentrationslager	(German) Concentration camp
Körözöt	A popular cheese spread made from goat or fresh cow's cheese mixed with sour cream, paprika, pepper and chives
Korrekt	(German) Correct
Kurzbach Lied	(German) Kurzbach song (Kurzbach is a village in Germany)
Lazarett	(German) Military camp hospital or sick bay

Mitzvot	(Hebrew) Good deeds
Nazi Kultur	(German) Nazi culture
Oneg Shabbat	(Hebrew) Observation of the Sabbath
Panzer	(German) Armoured tank
Partizans	Freedom fighters
Prügelstrafe	(German) Punishment by flogging or beating
Razzias	Raids
Raus	(German; abbreviation of Heraus) Get out
Reichsbahn	(German) German railroad or railway lines
Reichsführer	(German) A top-ranking administration post in the Nazi Party
Reichsprotektor	(German) Nazi government official in charge of a Reichsprotektorat
Reichsprotektorat	(German) A region not occupied by ethnic Germans but ruled by Nazi Germany
Rucksack	Backpack
Schälküche	(German) A room where the vegetables were peeled
Schnell, schnell	(German) Quickly, quickly
Shul	(Yiddish) Synagogue
SS Obersturmbannführer	(German) Equivalent rank to Lieutenant
SS Obersturnmführer	(German) Equivalent rank to Colonel

SS Hauptsturmführer	(German) Equivalent rank to Captain
SS Sturmbannführer	(German) Equivalent rank to Major
Stubenalteste	(German) A female prisoner placed in charge of the other women in her barracks
Štubova	(Polish) Slang for *Stubenalteste*
Sudeten Deutsche Partei	Pro-Geman party of Czech citizens of German origin
Sukkah	A roofless room where meals are consumed during the Sukkoth Festival.
Sukkoth	Jewish festival of tabernacles
Vodca	(Slovak) Leader
WIZO	Womens International Zionist Organisation
Yiskor	(Hebrew) Memorial prayer for deceased
Zyklon B	Gas used in the extermination chambers

Europe, showing camps featured in the text

International boundaries, 1933